Teaching STEM and Common Core with Mentor Texts

Collaborative Lesson Plans, K–5

Anastasia Suen and Shirley Duke

LIBRARIES UNLIMITED

AN IMPRINT OF ABC-CLIO, LLC

Santa Barbara, California • Denver, Colorado • Oxford, England

Library of Congress Cataloging-in-Publication Data

Suen, Anastasia.
   Teaching STEM and common core with mentor texts : collaborative lesson plans, K-5 / Anastasia Suen and Shirley Duke.
      pages   cm
   ISBN 978-1-61069-426-1 (pbk.) — ISBN 978-1-61069-597-8 (eBook)   1. Science—Study and teaching—United States.   2. Technology—Study and teaching—United States.   3. Engineering—Study and teaching—United States.   4. Mathematics—Study and teaching—United States.   5. Language arts (Elementary)—Curricula—United States.   6. Language arts (Elementary)—Standards—United States. 7. School librarian participation in curriculum planning—United States.   8. Libraries and teachers—United States.   I. Title.
   LB1585.S85   2014
   372.35'044—dc23   2013030161

ISBN: 978-1-61069-426-1
EISBN: 978-1-61069-597-8

18 17 16 15 14   1 2 3 4 5

This book is also available on the World Wide Web as an eBook.
Visit www.abc-clio.com for details.

Libraries Unlimited
An Imprint of ABC-CLIO, LLC

ABC-CLIO, LLC
130 Cremona Drive, P.O. Box 1911
Santa Barbara, California 93116-1911

This book is printed on acid-free paper ∞

Manufactured in the United States of America

All graphic organizers were designed by Aimée Suen.

Teaching STEM and Common Core
with Mentor Texts

Contents

PART II: Teaching Science in Your Library

Acknowledgments

We want to give a special thanks to all of the school librarians who field-tested these lessons, especially Allyson F. Cogan, Ann Schuster, April Reitnauer, Beth Roy, Carol Owen, Carolyn Bailey, Heidi Lose Keairns, Jennifer Koch, Leslie Senn, Leslie E. Sharbel, Linda Ann Wrins-Ryan, Marge Cox, and Theresa Mayer.

ATOS readability levels were determined by Renaissance Learning, Inc., who holds the copyright.

Lexile Levels were determined by Lexile® Framework For Reading by Meta-Metrics, who holds the copyright.

Use of the Common Core State Standards is permitted by the National Governors Association Center for Best Practices and the Council of Chief State School Officers. © Copyright 2010. National Governors Association Center for Best Practices and Council of Chief State School Officers. All rights reserved.

PART I

Teaching STEM in Your Library

Introduction

This book was written to bring the Common Core State Standards and science, technology, engineering, and math (STEM) together with books and lessons that can easily be done in the library and then extended into classrooms. It is our hope that these lessons will allow you to develop additional lessons from the books in your library and follow the pattern to continue teaching STEM topics in your library.

The book is divided by STEM subjects, and there are five library lessons for each subject based on a mentor text. Lessons for the collaborating teacher follow the library lessons, although these may also be done in the library. A suggested list of exemplary texts and the Common Core State Standards are included with each lesson.

All lessons begin with information about the mentor text, author, and pertinent reading information. Related subjects and grade levels show the range of grades for which the lesson is most suited and lead to the essential question about what the lesson teaches.

A unit summary provides an overview of what will take place in the lesson, and related vocabulary from the book is listed for use either in pre-teaching, with the collaborating teacher, or for related activities or lessons. After the unit summary, you will find a list of the Common Core State Standards met in this unit. Both English Language Arts and Mathematics standards are listed. An approximate lesson length suggests the amount of time needed to complete the entire lesson, and suggested breaks are included in the lesson itself.

A booktalk is provided to interest the students in the book, and a Book Time section allows for reading all or parts of the book and a general discussion. A titled lesson begins with a list of necessary materials and directions for lesson preparation ahead of time. Each lesson contains a graphic organizer (GO Chart) that can be used with the lesson. The steps of each lesson are listed, and time for reflection is built in. Two choices for assessing the lesson are provided. A second lesson that can be used with a collaborating teacher follows the same pattern and extends the concept learned in the library lesson.

Several extension activities suggest ways to delve deeper into the topic and provide alternate ideas that might be included in the lesson. Modifications for other grades show ways the lesson can be taught to students in the different grades. A list of differentiation strategies addresses extending or reining in the lesson to fit the needs of special populations: students on Individual Education Programs (IEPs), bilingual or English Language Learners, or gifted students. Resources from online and other related books covered by the lesson conclude the section. Because online resources are always changing, you can find a copy of the latest links in our online STEM folders (asuen.com/stem/ and shirleysmithduke.com/stem/).

The lessons were based on the standards for the highest grade level in the grouping. Since the standards are related, you can simplify the lesson slightly to fit a wide range of grades while remaining focused on the standards. The lessons were written to provide guidelines but are easily adaptable, and you can feel free to make them your own.

1
What is STEM?

While many people can identify the acronym STEM as meaning science, technology, engineering, and mathematics, the meaning of its totality becomes more difficult to pin down. Definitions abound and are frequently set within the context of the group doing the defining. A common definition states:

> STEM education is an interdisciplinary approach to learning where rigorous academic concepts are coupled with real-world lessons as students apply science, technology, engineering, and mathematics in contexts that make connections between school, community, work, and the global enterprise enabling the development of STEM literacy and with it the ability to compete in the new economy. (Tsupros, 2009)

Current education frequently puts science and mathematics at the forefront and includes engineering and technology when it fits the curriculum. STEM subjects are often taught in isolation, without reference to the other subjects. This compartmentalized approach brings up more questions about what STEM is. Is it a STEM program if only math or science is being taught? Or must all the subjects be included if it is to be called a STEM curriculum? Many questions remain as educators work to identify what STEM is and how it will fit into their state or national standards.

For now, STEM can be considered a new discipline—one based on integrating the four subjects. By bridging the four previously independent fields, this entity called STEM can then be taught by educators so that students are stimulated to learn how to problem solve, understand concepts, and use their knowledge in innovative ways.

Why STEM?

The last part of the previous definition brings up the question of the eroding ability of U.S. students to compete on the world stage in these academic areas. Enterprise today requires an advanced technical know-how and problem solving that wasn't necessary ten years ago. The need for a qualified STEM workforce is present now. Problems facing today's society include meeting energy needs, treating diseases and developing new medicines, dealing with the results of climate change, and the creation of innovations necessary to function successfully in a rapidly changing, global world. Education will have to prepare young people to address the changes facing their future. The workforce views STEM differently than the educational view of teaching students through a rigorous curriculum to be prepared for a highly specialized job in the fields; rather, STEM workforce needs innovative, creative thinkers who can solve problems. Industry today requires problem solvers that can quickly develop solutions in a cost-effective way.

In 2005, a coalition of businesses and technology associations outlined several steps needed in schools to continue American competitiveness in science and engineering. Their report urged Americans to improve the STEM disciplines and make it a national priority, to find a way to motive students to enter and study STEM fields, and to upgrade math and science teaching. A follow-up report in 2007 pushed for Congress to act on an agenda that would keep America able to succeed in a global economy.

Currently, there are no national STEM standards or certification for STEM teachers. There is a need to plan, write, and put into practice a STEM program that includes the necessary elements across the individual disciplines and that connects them in a meaningful and logical way. The Next Generation Science Standards are an attempt to address these needs.

STEM and Librarians

As STEM curricula are being developed, it falls on the educational system to work with children at an early age to incorporate the qualities necessary to excel in this field. Teaching STEM from kindergarten on is critical to the education of all children to address the need for people to be educated and well-equipped to develop and use the rapidly changing technology. Their skills will have to meet the demands of society while keeping the environment in a healthy balance.

Librarians can become a key component in STEM education, guiding and sparking interest through the books and technology inherent in their curriculum. Books provide a natural entry to all STEM subjects, and librarians possess a wide range of knowledge about them. By introducing students to all of the subjects, they can create a deeper interest in all the STEM disciplines.

By educating children from kindergarten through high school in content and the process skills that apply, as well as integrating problem-solving and creativity required to successfully carry out innovation from a young age, students will be prepared for the twenty-first century workforce and will be able to meet the challenges and changes sure to come in the future. Librarians have the opportunity to work with and interact with all the students in their schools. It becomes easy to be a STEM catalyst for young minds as they begin and move forward in their education, and you can make the difference.

As a librarian, you are an information specialist and highly qualified in what you do. The good news is that it isn't necessary for you to have a background in STEM fields to facilitate STEM education. You simply do what you have been trained to do.

You can direct people to STEM books and other resources available for the STEM subjects. You can increase the number of STEM books in your library. You can support learning in the STEM subjects.

Librarians provide a leadership role by collaborating with the classroom teachers and keeping them knowledgeable about the resources they can use to include STEM in their classes. Through you, the highly informative, technical STEM subjects become accessible to everyone with whom you work.

Common Core and Librarians

The Common Core standards set the expectations for elementary and secondary schools across the United States in order to allow students to graduate with the knowledge and skills they need to further their education and compete in the workplace. Currently, forty-five states, the District of Columbia, four territories, and the Department of Defense Education have adopted the Common Core learning expectations. The American Association of School Librarians (AASL) has found that their standards correlate closely with the Common Core skills. The AASL's "Crosswalk" has lined up the benchmarks of both, showing the relationship of the sets of skills.

The Common Core Standards emphasize reading across the curriculum, including the content areas. Librarians and media specialists can facilitate the teaching of these standards through their information literacy skills and critical thinking using books, technology, and their library.

Informational texts will become increasingly important to young learners, and the percentage of nonfiction reading increases as the students move through high school. Students will be required to read a variety of texts and learn to read, research, interpret, write, and present the information in an analytical or critical way. In addition to books, librarians will need to find databases and online resources to supplement the library books.

Librarians make a natural transition between inquiry and learning to young learners. They have the means to encourage inquiry and teach strategies that allow students to find, analyze, and synthesize the information they encounter. Additionally, the librarian provides a natural point for collaboration with the classroom teachers and can initiate this collaboration using the Common Core Standards as the starting point.

Librarians have the opportunity to introduce students to the vast amount of knowledge contained in nonfiction and through teaching library skills; they can enlarge upon and expand the ways young people learn.

2
Addressing Text Complexity

With the advent of the Common Core State Standards comes a new focus on text complexity. Measuring the complexity of a text is not new. Software programs to analyze text complexity have existed for years. These programs analyze a given text and create a reading level score. Each program has its own formula for determining the reading level of any given text. Word and sentence length are taken into account; in most cases, long words and long sentences will be given a higher reading level, while short words and short sentences will be given a lower reading level. As a result, each word in the English language has been given a reading level, so that there are kindergarten words, first grade words, second grade words, etc.

At the same time, these reading level software programs also take into account the fact that elementary school students are still learning to read. What a child can understand and what a child can read independently are not the same. At the independent reading level, a child can read a given text on his own—no adult assistance is required.

In the classroom, we often work with students at their instructional level, where a child can read with help. For a book to be at a student's instructional level, the child must be able to read 95 percent of the words without help. (Yes, this is an "A" grade!) When the reading level drops below 95 percent, the book falls into the student's frustration level, an event we want to avoid at all costs. This is not the message we want to send about the library, reading, or STEM.

Audio books may be one way to work around low-level readers. Even children who cannot read at all can understand the spoken word. (This is why picture books have sophisticated language and beginning readers do not. Beginning readers are meant to be read by students without adult assistance.)

The Lexile® Framework For Reading by MetaMetrics is one software leveling program. It lists a number for the reading level, but some books also have a two-letter code in front of that number. On the Lexile Codes page of their website, they explain, "Word frequency and sentence length—the two text characteristics that determine a Lexile measure—do not describe all of the content of a book." So codes were added to provide context.

Most of the picture books in your library are AD (Adult Directed) because they are written for children who do not read on their own yet. Picture books are read *by* adults *to* children.

The IG (Illustrated Guide) label is given to "factoid" books like the DK Eyewitness series. These lushly illustrated reference books have short factoids next to each photograph and illustration, but the facts can be read in any order.

You will also see GN (Graphic Novel) for books that are written as "comic" books. The only thing is, not all comic books are novels. (The proper name for these books is "graphica," but that name has not come into common use yet.)

Although there are many reading level software programs, you will only see two referenced in this book: ATOS and Lexile. This was done for two reasons. The first is easy access. Both ATOS and Lexile are free to anyone searching the web. The Lexile website has a "Find a Book" feature that allows you to search by level or by book title. The ATOS levels can be found online by searching the AR™ Book Finder website. (AR™ is the abbreviation for Accelerated Reader, which is owned by Renaissance Learning, Inc.) In addition to the ATOS reading level for a given book, the AR™ Book Finder site also lists the number of words in the book. (AR quizzes must be purchased, but the reading level listings are free online.)

The second reason that ATOS and Lexile are used in this book is that both of these measures were used in a Common Core text complexity study—the "Supplemental Information for Appendix A of the Common Core State Standards for English Language Arts and Literacy: New Research on Text Complexity."

Researchers cross-referenced the results to create a new "Common Core Band" chart. (You can see the complete chart and more in this study on the Common Core webpage.) For our purposes, here are the K–5 results for ATOS and Lexile.

You'll notice that there isn't a band for kindergarten and first grade. This is the age when students are learning to read. The study said that books for these beginning readers often had features that made them difficult to assess.

As children learn to read, they move through four stages: emergent, early, transitional, and fluent. The first two stages usually occur in kindergarten and first grade. As students begin to transition, they stop relying on the pictures to tell them what is happening in the words. It is at the end of the transitional stage that the text complexity grade bands begin.

The final common core band level (not shown here) is eleventh–CCR. As you know from reading the standards, CCR is the acronym used for College and Career Readiness. This makes the text complexity chart end with the Common Core State Standard's ultimate goal. The final level of text complexity is equivalent to the first year of college or workforce training.

Figure 2-1.   New Common Core Text Complexity Bands

Common Core Band	ATOS	The Lexile Framework®
2nd–3rd	2.75–5.14	420–820
4th–5th	4.97–7.03	740–1010

The reality of the classroom is that every student has a different reading level. In the library, you will encounter kindergarteners who read at second grade level and fifth graders who read at second grade level. Finding books to meet everyone's needs is always a challenge.

To help you meet this challenge, all of the STEM mentor texts in this book have either an ATOS or a Lexile level (or both) listed. The mentor texts have their levels listed at the beginning of the chapter. At the end of each chapter are five exemplar texts with their reading levels listed. The exemplars extend the lesson by allowing you to recommend other books for further reading. You can also use them to create a book display in the library.

Of course, there are many great STEM books that are not listed in this volume. Our goal was to highlight recent books about the topics in the lessons. Classic books like David Schwartz's *How Much is a Million?* are not listed here. Books that are so new that they don't have ATOS or Lexile levels yet, like *Seymour Simon's Extreme Oceans*, aren't listed either. A book list is always a moment in time. (You can subscribe to the STEM Friday blog to stay up-to-date on the latest STEM books.)

3

A Closer Look at the Standards

The new Common Core State Standards are exit standards. They are goals to reach by the end of the school year. Your classroom teachers have a grade-specific bullet point list for each standard. The standards are listed on a continuum from kindergarten to college.

In this book, we will use the anchor standards as our guides. The anchor standards are "big picture" standards. They will guide you as you guide your students to answer the essential question in each mentor text unit.

The STEM books recommended in this guide have both language arts and mathematics elements, so we will use both the English Language Arts (ELA) and Mathematics standards.

As you use the lessons in this book, you'll notice that there are dozens of standards for each unit shown in the sidebars. This is because these units are written for the entire school. We want you to be able to use these STEM lessons with every student who visits your library. There are K–2 books with modifications for grades 3–5 and grades 3–5 books with modifications for K–2. Each unit also has a differentiation section for your special populations: students on IEPs, bilingual or ELL students, and gifted students. As you meet the needs of these students in the library, you will be working with all of these standards.

You will also meet many standards in a single unit because of the active and collaborative nature of the lessons. Students won't just sit and listen. They will read, research, and conduct experiments in the library. This means they will be meeting the standards for reading, writing, speaking and listening, language, and mathematics while they are working with you in the library.

To complete the hands-on lessons you teach in the library, students will need to practice their language arts and mathematics skills. Over time, these learning experiences will help students develop knowledge, skill, and understanding. Literacy is a shared responsibility.

You can download a copy of these standards on the Common Core State Standards website. (Use of the Common Core State Standards is permitted by the National Governors Association Center for Best Practices and the Council of Chief State School Officers.)

Common Core State Standards for English Language Arts

The English Language Arts are divided into four different areas: reading, writing, speaking and listening, and language. Each area of study has its own standards.

Common Core Anchor Standards for Reading

Key Ideas and Details

1. Read closely to determine what the text says explicitly and to make logical inferences from it; cite specific textual evidence when writing or speaking to support conclusions drawn from the text.
2. Determine central ideas or themes of a text and analyze their development; summarize the key supporting details and ideas.
3. Analyze how and why individuals, events, and ideas develop and interact over the course of a text.

Craft and Structure

4. Interpret words and phrases as they are used in a text, including determining technical, connotative, and figurative meanings, and analyze how specific word choices shape meaning or tone.
5. Analyze the structure of texts, including how specific sentences, paragraphs, and larger portions of the text (e.g., a section, chapter, scene, or stanza) relate to each other and the whole.
6. Assess how point of view or purpose shapes the content and style of a text.

Integration of Knowledge and Ideas

7. Integrate and evaluate content presented in diverse media and formats, including visually and quantitatively, as well as in words.
8. Delineate and evaluate the argument and specific claims in a text, including the validity of the reasoning as well as the relevance and sufficiency of the evidence.
9. Analyze how two or more texts address similar themes or topics in order to build knowledge or to compare the approaches the authors take.

Range of Reading and Level of Text Complexity

10. Read and comprehend complex literary and informational texts independently and proficiently.

Common Core Anchor Standards for Writing

Text Types and Purposes

1. Write arguments to support claims in an analysis of substantive topics or texts, using valid reasoning and relevant and sufficient evidence.
2. Write informative/explanatory texts to examine and convey complex ideas and information clearly and accurately through the effective selection, organization, and analysis of content.

3. Write narratives to develop real or imagined experiences or events using effective technique, well-chosen details, and well-structured event sequences.

Production and Distribution of Writing

4. Produce clear and coherent writing in which the development, organization, and style are appropriate to task, purpose, and audience.
5. Develop and strengthen writing as needed by planning, revising, editing, rewriting, or trying a new approach.
6. Use technology, including the Internet, to produce and publish writing and to interact and collaborate with others.

Research to Build and Present Knowledge

7. Conduct short as well as more sustained research projects based on focused questions, demonstrating understanding of the subject under investigation.
8. Gather relevant information from multiple print and digital sources, assess the credibility and accuracy of each source, and integrate the information while avoiding plagiarism.
9. Draw evidence from literary or informational texts to support analysis, reflection, and research.

Range of Writing

10. Write routinely over extended time frames (time for research, reflection, and revision) and shorter time frames (a single sitting or a day or two) for a range of tasks, purposes, and audiences.

Common Core Anchor Standards for Speaking and Listening

Comprehension and Collaboration

1. Prepare for and participate effectively in a range of conversations and collaborations with diverse partners, building on others' ideas and expressing their own clearly and persuasively.
2. Integrate and evaluate information presented in diverse media and formats, including visually, quantitatively, and orally.
3. Evaluate a speaker's point of view, reasoning, and use of evidence and rhetoric.

Presentation of Knowledge and Ideas

4. Present information, findings, and supporting evidence such that listeners can follow the line of reasoning and the organization, development, and style are appropriate to task, purpose, and audience.
5. Make strategic use of digital media and visual displays of data to express information and enhance understanding of presentations.
6. Adapt speech to a variety of contexts and communicative tasks, demonstrating command of formal English when indicated or appropriate.

Common Core Anchor Standards for Language

Conventions of Standard English

1. Demonstrate command of the conventions of standard English grammar and usage when writing or speaking.
2. Demonstrate command of the conventions of standard English capitalization, punctuation, and spelling when writing.

Knowledge of Language

3. Apply knowledge of language to understand how language functions in different contexts, to make effective choices for meaning or style, and to comprehend more fully when reading or listening.

Vocabulary Acquisition and Use

4. Determine or clarify the meaning of unknown and multiple-meaning words and phrases by using context clues, analyzing meaningful word parts, and consulting general and specialized reference materials, as appropriate.
5. Demonstrate understanding of figurative language, word relationships, and nuances in word meanings.
6. Acquire and use accurately a range of general academic and domain-specific words and phrases sufficient for reading, writing, speaking, and listening at the college and career readiness level; demonstrate independence in gathering vocabulary knowledge when encountering an unknown term important to comprehension or expression.

Common Core State Standards for Mathematics

The Common Core Mathematics Standards cover two areas: mathematical practice and mathematical content. Mathematical Practices apply to each grade. Mathematical Content, on the other hand, can be grade-specific. The content standards for each grade are grouped by math domains.

Some math domains are only taught in certain grades. Counting and cardinality, for example, are only taught in kindergarten. Other math domains, like geometry, build as the grades rise. What students learn in each domain builds on what they have learned in previous grades.

Common Core Mathematical Practices

1. Make sense of problems and persevere in solving them.
2. Reason abstractly and quantitatively.
3. Construct viable arguments and critique the reasoning of others.
4. Model with mathematics.
5. Use appropriate tools strategically.
6. Attend to precision.
7. Look for and make use of structure.
8. Look for and express regularity in repeated reasoning.

Grade K Mathematical Content

Counting and Cardinality

- Know number names and the count sequence.
- Count to tell the number of objects.
- Compare numbers.

Operations and Algebraic Thinking

- Understand addition as putting together and adding to, and understand subtraction as taking apart and taking from.

Number and Operations in Base Ten

- Work with numbers 11–19 to gain foundations for place value.

Measurement and Data

- Describe and compare measurable attributes.
- Classify objects and count the number of objects in categories.

Geometry

- Identify and describe shapes.
- Analyze, compare, create, and compose shapes.

Grade 1 Mathematical Content

Operations and Algebraic Thinking

- Represent and solve problems involving addition and subtraction.
- Understand and apply properties of operations and the relationship between addition and subtraction.
- Add and subtract within 20.
- Work with addition and subtraction equations.

Number and Operations in Base Ten

- Extend the counting sequence.
- Understand place value.
- Use place value understanding and properties of operations to add and subtract.

Measurement and Data

- Measure lengths indirectly and by iterating length units.
- Tell and write time.
- Represent and interpret data.

Geometry

- Reason with shapes and their attributes.

Grade 2 Mathematical Content

Operations and Algebraic Thinking

- Represent and solve problems involving addition and subtraction.
- Add and subtract within 20.
- Work with equal groups of objects to gain foundations for multiplication.

Number and Operations in Base Ten

- Understand place value.
- Use place value understanding and properties of operations to add and subtract.

Measurement and Data

- Measure and estimate lengths in standard units.
- Relate addition and subtraction to length.
- Work with time and money.
- Represent and interpret data.

Geometry

- Reason with shapes and their attributes.

Grade 3 Mathematical Content

Operations and Algebraic Thinking

- Represent and solve problems involving multiplication and division.
- Understand properties of multiplication and the relationship between multiplication and division.
- Multiply and divide within 100.
- Solve problems involving the four operations, and identify and explain patterns in arithmetic.

Number and Operations in Base Ten

- Use place value understanding and properties of operations to perform multi-digit arithmetic.

Number and Operations—Fractions

- Develop understanding of fractions as numbers.

Measurement and Data

- Solve problems involving measurement and estimation of intervals of time, liquid volumes, and masses of objects.
- Represent and interpret data.
- Geometric measurement: understand concepts of area and relate area to multiplication and to addition.
- Geometric measurement: recognize perimeter as an attribute of plane figures and distinguish between linear and area measures.

Geometry

- Reason with shapes and their attributes.

Grade 4 Mathematical Content

Operations and Algebraic Thinking

- Use the four operations with whole numbers to solve problems.
- Gain familiarity with factors and multiples.
- Generate and analyze patterns.

Number and Operations in Base Ten

- Generalize place value understanding for multi-digit whole numbers.
- Use place value understanding and properties of operations to perform multi-digit arithmetic.

Number and Operations—Fractions

- Extend understanding of fraction equivalence and ordering.
- Build fractions from unit fractions by applying and extending previous understandings of operations on whole numbers.
- Understand decimal notation for fractions, and compare decimal fractions.

Measurement and Data

- Solve problems involving measurement and conversion of measurements from a larger unit to a smaller unit.
- Represent and interpret data.
- Geometric measurement: understand concepts of angles and measure angles.

Geometry

- Draw and identify lines and angles, and classify shapes by properties of their lines and angles.

Grade 5 Mathematical Content

Operations and Algebraic Thinking

- Write and interpret numerical expressions.
- Analyze patterns and relationships.

Number and Operations in Base Ten

- Understand the place value system.
- Perform operations with multi-digit whole numbers and with decimals to hundredths.

Number and Operations—Fractions

- Use equivalent fractions as a strategy to add and subtract fractions.
- Apply and extend previous understandings of multiplication and division to multiply and divide fractions.

Measurement and Data

- Convert like measurement units within a given measurement system.
- Represent and interpret data.
- Geometric measurement: understand concepts of volume and relate volume to multiplication and to addition.

Geometry

- Graph points on the coordinate plane to solve real-world and mathematical problems.
- Classify two-dimensional figures into categories based on their properties.

4 How to Use This Book

To demonstrate how to use this book, we've added a "bonus" technology unit to this guide. (In the rest of the book, each area of STEM will have five mentor text units.)

✎ A unit begins with an overview of the mentor text. Each area of STEM has a different icon so you can see at a glance where you are in the book. Science lessons have a beaker, technology lessons have a computer mouse, engineering lessons have a gear, and mathematics lessons have a ruler.

 A "Bonus" Demonstration Lesson

Enterprise Stem

By Shirley Duke. Rourke Publishing, 2012. 48p. (9781617417818)

Grade Level: 3–5 *(Grades K–2 with modifications)*
ATOS Reading Level: 6.5
Dewey: 500
Subject Area: technology, science, social studies

✎ An essential question guides students throughout the unit.

Essential Question: What recent changes have taken place in technology we use every day?

✎ The unit summary is an overview of all the lessons you can use with the mentor text.

Unit Summary: Students will examine the essential question, "What recent changes have taken place in technology we use every day?" They will discuss the kinds of

Common Core State Standards

(49 total)

✎ As you work with students in the library each day, you are helping them meet many Common Core State Standards. In the sidebar for each unit, you will see a list of the standards met in that unit. At the top of the sidebar is the total number of standards met. This is followed by a listing of the Anchors Standards for English

Language Arts and Mathematics taught in the unit.

Reading Standards (9)

✐ *The English Language Arts (ELA) Anchor Standards are listed first. The standards are divided into strands. The ELA strands are Reading, Writing, Speaking and Listening, and Language.*

Key Ideas and Details

1. Read closely to determine what the text says explicitly and to make logical inferences from it; cite specific textual evidence when writing or speaking to support conclusions drawn from the text.

2. Determine central ideas or themes of a text and analyze their development; summarize the key supporting details and ideas.

3. Analyze how and why individuals, events, and ideas develop and interact over the course of a text.

Craft and Structure

4. Interpret words and phrases as they are used in a text, including determining technical, connotative, and figurative meanings, and analyze how specific word choices shape meaning or tone.

Integration of Knowledge and Ideas

7. Integrate and evaluate content presented in diverse media and for-

technology they use currently and research information about the history and development of one of those forms. Students will use a list of suggestions to guide their research about the chosen kind of technology. They will then organize their information and use technology to create a class presentation in which the other students will note the important aspects of that technology development and write a question about it.

✐ *Important vocabulary words are listed at the beginning of the unit.*

Vocabulary: biomaterials, bioremediation, communication, condensed, data, digital, emissions, environmental scientists, fingerprinting, genes, GPS (global positioning systems), hybrid, microbes, military, monitor, nanotechnology, precision, processors, quantum computing, robotic, satellites, simulations, virtual

✐ *Each unit is divided into several lessons.*

Approximate lesson time: three class periods

✐ *You can use this booktalk with your students.*

Booktalk: In the future, you might have a job that we haven't heard of today. Technology is taking scientific knowledge and using it in a practical way. It is often used in industry, which means a certain branch of business involved in making things. Technology gives us ways to improve or change how the things we use work. It lets us do or make something in a better way. What sorts of technology are we talking about? Take a look at the book *Enterprise STEM*.

✐ *Follow up the booktalk with these activities.*

Book Time

1. Share the booktalk for *Enterprise STEM* (above). Read Chapters 4 and 5.
2. Ask the students to name some things they use every day. Write the list on a chart.
3. Read the list and add a "T" to each item that includes technology.

4. Point out and add to the list any of the following that are not already included: telephone, television, photo albums, written communication, computers, maps, keyboards, books, board games, radio, and cars.

✎ *After the discussion you can do the library activity (below) or you can end this class period with check out and save the activity for another class period.*

 Library Activity

Early Technology

I. Materials: list of items students use every day, computers, reference books relating to development or history of different technologies, graphic organizer

✎ *The graphic organizers are listed alphabetically by book title in the appendix. Make a copy for each student to guide and organize research.*

II. Instructions
   1. Tell the students they will be investigating the early forms of the technology they use today.
   2. Have them silently review the list you've made during the booktalk and choose one form of technology. Ask them to write it down.
   3. Tell the students that they will research an early form of their chosen technology and present the information they learn in a way that incorporates technology in a 3-minute presentation. This may include PowerPoint presentations, audio or video recordings, pictures, or any other technology available to them. Decide if you want the students to work individually or in small groups.
III. Procedure
   1. Tell the students that they need to look up and find information that must include:
      a. an early inventor who developed that technology
      b. description of what the early product looked like

mats, including visually and quantitatively, as well as in words.

8. Delineate and evaluate the argument and specific claims in a text, including the validity of the reasoning as well as the relevance and sufficiency of the evidence.

Range of Reading and Level of Text Complexity

10. Read and comprehend complex literary and informational texts independently and proficiently.

Writing Standards (9)

✎ *The English Language Arts Anchor Standards apply to all grades, from kindergarten to CCR (Career and College Readiness). That is the goal of these standards, to prepare students for their first year of college or career.*

Text Types and Purposes

1. Write arguments to support claims in an analysis of substantive topics or texts, using valid reasoning and relevant and sufficient evidence.

2. Write informative/explanatory texts to examine and convey complex ideas and information clearly and accurately through the effective selection, organization, and analysis of content.

Production and Distribution of Writing

4. Produce clear and coherent writing in which the development, organization, and style are appropriate to task, purpose, and audience.

5. Develop and strengthen writing as needed by planning, revising, editing, rewriting, or trying a new approach.

6. Use technology, including the Internet, to produce and publish writing and to interact and collaborate with others.

✎ *The research component is especially important in the library. You have been trained to help both students and teachers with this English Language Arts Anchor Standard.*

Research to Build and Present Knowledge

7. Conduct short as well as more sustained research projects based on focused questions, demonstrating understanding of the subject under investigation.

8. Gather relevant information from multiple print and digital sources, assess the credibility and accuracy of each source, and integrate the information while avoiding plagiarism.

9. Draw evidence from literary or informational

    c. its size then

    d. changes it underwent

    e. an explanation about why they think the inventor first made it or why they think it was needed

2. Ask them to keep a list of important dates relating to their technology to use later.

3. Have students research and locate information to use to create their presentations. Allow them enough time to research and find their facts.

4. Using their recorded information, students will present their findings to the group.

5. Listening students will record the most important idea from the presentation and write one question that came to mind during each presentation.

6. Have the students ask one of the questions they wrote during the presentations. Have the presenter or presenting group answer it.

7. Each student will then write an answer relating to the essential question.

IV. Reflect

1. Ask the students to review their presentation silently.

2. Then have them individually write down what was good about their presentation in a paragraph.

3. Next have them write down any changes they could have included that would help improve it.

V. Assessment

Choice 1

Use the individual or group presentations to assess their work.

Choice 2

Have students write a concluding statement about why they chose this particular form of technology to explore and the value of their chosen technology. Support their answers using information from their presentation.

Collaborative Teacher Activity

Technology Timeline

🖉 *Each chapter also has a collaborative lesson for your classroom teachers. (You can also teach this lesson in the library if there is no cooperating teacher who is able to do it. This gives you an extra lesson for each mentor text.)*

I. Materials: paper for the timeline, rulers, computers, reference books relating to development or history of different technologies, individual presentations

II. Instructions
1. Tell the students they will develop a simple timeline detailing their technology.
2. Have them draw a 100-cm line and divide it into 10 cm sections using a longer line.
3. Tell them they must include 5 important dates relating to the technology they used in the library presentation. Remind them to refer to the dates they collected during the library research.

III. Activity
1. Instruct the students to label their timeline using dates by decades that best fit with their technological invention. For example, one timeline might begin with 1880, 1890, 1900, and so on until the final line is labeled 1990. Another student may need to begin with 1930 and end with 2030, depending on the origin of the invention.
2. Estimate the distance between decades to mark each individual date they have chosen.
3. Label each of the dates with the achievement or progress.
4. Develop an icon to illustrate each chosen date and add it to their timeline.
5. Provide time for the students to create their timelines in the development of their technology.

IV. Reflection
1. Post the timelines or have each student display it on his or her desk. Allow the students

texts to support analysis, reflection, and research.

Range of Writing

10. Write routinely over extended time frames (time for research, reflection, and revision) and shorter time frames (a single sitting or a day or two) for a range of tasks, purposes, and audiences.

Speaking and Listening Standards (5)

🖉 *Collaboration is another key component of your work with both students and teachers. You may already be working on this English Language Arts Anchor Standard daily!*

Comprehension and Collaboration

1. Prepare for and participate effectively in a range of conversations and collaborations with diverse partners, building on others' ideas and expressing their own clearly and persuasively.

2. Integrate and evaluate information presented in diverse media and formats, including visually, quantitatively, and orally.

Presentation of Knowledge and Ideas

4. Present information, findings, and supporting evidence such that listeners can follow the line of reasoning and the organization, development, and style are appropriate to

task, purpose, and audience.

5. Make strategic use of digital media and visual displays of data to express information and enhance understanding of presentations.

6. Adapt speech to a variety of contexts and communicative tasks, demonstrating command of formal English when indicated or appropriate.

Language Standards (4)

🖉 *Communicating with your students in the library every day allows you to help them learn new words. It also gives you the opportunity to model the conventions of Standards of English. This applies to both native and non-native speakers.*

Conventions of Standard English

1. Demonstrate command of the conventions of standard English grammar and usage when writing or speaking.

2. Demonstrate command of the conventions of standard English capitalization, punctuation, and spelling when writing.

Vocabulary Acquisition and Use

4. Determine or clarify the meaning of unknown and multiple-meaning words and phrases by using

to move around to each desk and view the timelines presented.

2. When they return to their desk, have them review their own timeline. Ask them to list the good things they saw as they walked around the room. Write their comments on a chart or the board. Then have them individually write bulleted points about what they might do to improve their own timeline.

V. Assessment

1. Review the timelines to see if each student included five important events in the development of the chosen technology.

2. Ask the students to write a paragraph that highlights the development of their technology. Support their statements with the timeline dates they used.

Extension Activities

🖉 *Use these activities to extend the lesson in a later session.*

1. Have the students read further about the inventor of their technology and write a short summary of that information.

2. Create a visual using information from their own timeline to show the important facts in another way. This can include charts, graphs, diagrams, or pictures presenting the information. Share them with the class.

3. Look up jobs that involve technology. Make a list and write a short definition of each job.

4. After reading the book, have the students write a short description of the main idea of the book. Use the phrase, "I am a technology specialist. I know that _____."

Modifications for Grades K–2

🖉 *Modify these lessons for a different grade level.*

1. Assign topics to the groups and collect the information in their research groups.

2. Use the research note-taking graphic organizer page in groups or pairs to guide their search using Step 3.1 from the lesson.

3. Give them a list of relevant research materials and resources related to their topic.

4. Have the students prepare a shorter presentation using technology or present their findings using posters, in writing, or orally.

Differentiation strategies:

✐ *Differentiate the lessons for special populations: students on IEPs, bilingual or ELL students, or gifted students.*

1. Discuss, define, or review the vocabulary before reading the book. Point out examples of how the words were used.
2. Identify or list the links that are available to help students locate their timeline information.
3. Prepare a vocabulary note-taking page and then read the chapters a second time. Stop and guide the students as they take notes for each energy source.
4. Discuss the possible means of using technology available in your media center.
5. Use strategic grouping by working in small groups.
6. Allow students to present their information orally or in a written paper.

✐ *Use these online resources with your students.*

Resources:

Audiocasts about five scientists
http://www.fi.edu/learn/case-files/audiocasts.html

Histories of different technologies
http://transition.fcc.gov/cgb/kidszone/history.html

Famous people and events in history
http://www.history-timelines.org.uk/events-time lines/12-technology-timeline.htm

✐ *You can also find these links at asuen.com/stem/ and shirleysmithduke.com/stem/*

History of communication
http://inventors.about.com/library/inventors/bl_ history_of_communication.htm

context clues, analyzing meaningful word parts, and consulting general and specialized reference materials, as appropriate.

6. Acquire and use accurately a range of general academic and domain-specific words and phrases sufficient for reading, writing, speaking, and listening.

Mathematical Practices (3)

✐ *We use mathematical practices every day when we take what we know and apply math to solve problems in real life.*

1. Make sense of problems and persevere in solving them.

2. Reason abstractly and quantitatively.

4. Model with mathematics.

5. Use appropriate tools strategically.

6. Attend to precision.

7. Look for and make use of structure.

Mathematical Content (15)

✐ *Which mathematical content we use depends on the problem we are trying to solve.*

Operations and Algebraic Thinking

• Use the four operations with whole numbers to solve problems.

• Gain familiarity with factors and multiples.

• Generate and analyze patterns.

• Use place value understanding and properties of operations to perform multi-digit arithmetic.

Number and Operations in Base Ten

• Extend the counting sequence.

• Understand place value.

• Generalize place value understanding for multi-digit whole numbers.

Measurement and Data

• Describe and compare measurable attributes.

• Classify objects and count the number of objects in categories.

• Tell and write time.

• Measure and estimate lengths in standard units.

• Solve problems involving measurement and estimation of intervals of time, liquid volumes, and masses of objects.

• Solve problems involving measurement and

Fun technology facts
http://www.sciencekids.co.nz/sciencefacts/technology.html

The Science Spot with computers and technology
http://sciencespot.net/Pages/kdztech.html

✎ *If you find that an online resource is broken, please notify us so we can replace it with a new one.*

Exemplar Texts:

✎ *Create a book display or use these exemplars to extend the lessons.*

Cool Tech: Gadgets, Games, Robots, and the Digital World.
By Clive Gifford. DK Pub., 2011. 128p. (9780756682705)
Grade Level: 4–9
Lexile Level: IG 1190L
Dewey: 621.381

Game On: Have You Got What It Takes to Be a Video Game Developer?
By Lisa Thompson. Compass Point Books, 2010. 48p. (9780756542085)
Grade Level: 4–8
ATOS Reading Level: 6.7
Lexile Level: IG 990L
Dewey: 794.8

✎ *The grade level and reading level for each book is also listed.*

Steve Jobs.
By Joanne Mattern. Children's Press, 2013. 32p. (9780531247396)
Grade Level: 1–2
ATOS Reading Level: 3.2
Lexile Level: 560L
Dewey: 921

Technology.
By Clive Gifford. Scholastic, 2012. 112p. (9780531229606)
Grade Level: 3–9
Lexile Level: NC 1080L
Dewey: 600

Technology: A Byte-Size World.
Dan Green. Kingfisher, 2012. 128p. (9780753468197)
Grade Level: 4–8
Lexile Level: 1010L
Dewey: 600

🖉 *A master title list of all the books listed in this guide can be found in the appendix.*

conversion of measurements from a larger unit to a smaller unit.

• Convert like measurement units within a given measurement system.

• Represent and interpret data.

PART II

Teaching Science in Your Library

Science is . . .

Definition: Science is a system that provides a way to acquire knowledge by observing and experimenting.

Background

The word *science* comes from the Latin word for "knowledge" or "to know." The knowledge in science comes from investigating by means of a process called the scientific method. This method involves asking a question, observing and researching information already known about the question, forming a hypothesis (answer based on the knowledge at hand about what will result from the experiment), experimentation under controlled circumstances, recording results, drawing conclusions, and presenting those conclusions. The facts and observations are then used to determine and set up laws and principles that make up the natural world.

Pure science differs from applied science, which involves engineering and/or technology to solve the problems and requirements of human needs. Pure or natural science studies the natural world. The field includes life science, or biology; chemistry; physics (physical science in the early grades); and earth science.

5
Animals and the Environment

By Jennifer Boothroyd. Lerner, 2008. 24p. (9780822586029)

Grade Level: K–3 *(Grades 4–5 with modifications)*
ATOS Reading Level: 2.3
Lexile Level: 380
Dewey: 591.7
Subject Area: science

Essential Question: Why do animals live in different environments?

Unit Summary: Students will examine the essential question, "Why do animals live in different environments?" In small groups, they will read and research information about a specific animal and use the text features from the books to locate facts about their animal and why it lives in a specific environment. Using their combined information, the students will create a diagram or other text feature to illustrate the information they have gathered. They will include at least one animal adaptation that enables it to live in its specific habitat. Students will post their text features and will move around the room to read them.

Vocabulary: adapt, animals, endangered, environment, extinct, giraffes, ground, million, monkeys, population, prairie dogs, rodents, sharp

Approximate lesson time: one to two class periods

Common Core State Standards (41 total)

Reading Standards (7)

Key Ideas and Details

1. Read closely to determine what the text says explicitly and to make logical inferences from it; cite specific textual evidence when writing or speaking to support conclusions drawn from the text.

2. Determine central ideas or themes of a text and analyze their development; summarize the key supporting details and ideas.

3. Analyze how and why individuals, events, and ideas develop and interact over the course of a text.

Craft and Structure

4. Interpret words and phrases as they are used in a text, including determining technical, connotative, and figurative meanings, and analyze how specific word choices shape meaning or tone.

Integration of Knowledge and Ideas

7. Integrate and evaluate content presented in diverse media and formats, including visually and quantitatively, as well as in words.

8. Delineate and evaluate the argument and specific claims in a text, including the validity of the reasoning as well as the relevance and sufficiency of the evidence.

Range of Reading and Level of Text Complexity

10. Read and comprehend complex literary and informational texts independently and proficiently.

Writing Standards (9)

Text Types and Purposes

1. Write arguments to support claims in an analysis of substantive topics or texts, using valid reasoning and relevant and sufficient evidence.

2. Write informative/explanatory texts to examine and convey complex ideas and information clearly and accu-

Booktalk: Nonliving things are not alive. That includes rocks, water, and toasters. Living things are alive. So what do living things need in order to live? Living things need space, food, and water. They need a place to have babies. They have to eat and drink to stay alive. Think about the animals that you see every day. Where do they live? Animals live almost everywhere there's space for them and where they can get food and water. That is called their environment. Let's take a look at all the different places animals live and some of the things they do there by reading *Animals and the Environment*.

Book Time

1. Share the booktalk for *Animals and the Environment* (above).
2. Tell the students to listen for the names of the different kinds of animals you'll read about.
3. Read the book straight through.
4. Ask the students to name the animals they remembered from the book. List them on a chart where everyone can see them.

Library Activity

Feature This Animal

I. Materials: pencil and paper, selection of books about various animals, encyclopedias or animal references, graphic organizer
II. Instructions
    1. Divide the class into groups of two or three students each.
    2. Tell the groups that they will use different books to locate information about a specific animal and its habitat. They will read about the animal and find three text features used in the book to help understand the information. Then they will work together to create their own diagram to convey two to three facts about their animal and its environment, or the surroundings in which it lives. They will also include a section to show or tell how their text features provided information or reflected its use in the diagram.

3. They will present their diagram and tell an interesting fact about their animal and why it lives in that environment to the class.

III. Procedure

1. Pull relevant animal books ahead of time. Which animals you choose will depend on your collection. Select animals that live in a variety of environments.

2. Ask the students if they know what a text feature is. Tell them it is something that helps them more easily notice or learn about the facts in a book. Review examples of text features from some books.

3. Show them *Animals and the Environment*. Go back through the book and identify the text features: title on title page, bolded words, a graph, title for additional information, fact page, a glossary, and an index.

🖉 *Suggested lesson break.*

4. Discuss the items listed in Step 3 and what each helps them understand. Then direct them to the features they might look for as they read about their animal. Talk about the kinds of ways they could present their information as a diagram. Use some of your library books to show specific examples of a diagram.

5. Review their assignment and let them move to their groups. Assign an animal or let them choose one from the books you've pulled. Tell them they will make one diagram, but everyone needs to write down the two or three facts they agree to use.

6. Allow enough time for the students to complete the assignment.

7. Conduct the presentations and post the diagrams around the library area.

8. Discuss the things animals need to live and what helps them live where they live.

9. Answer the essential question.

IV. Reflect

1. Ask the students to think over their presentation and look at the facts they found. Read over them silently.

rately through the effective selection, organization, and analysis of content.

Production and Distribution of Writing

4. Produce clear and coherent writing in which the development, organization, and style are appropriate to task, purpose, and audience.

5. Develop and strengthen writing as needed by planning, revising, editing, rewriting, or trying a new approach.

6. Use technology, including the Internet, to produce and publish writing and to interact and collaborate with others.

Research to Build and Present Knowledge

7. Conduct short as well as more sustained research projects based on focused questions, demonstrating understanding of the subject under investigation.

8. Gather relevant information from multiple print and digital sources, assess the credibility and accuracy of each source, and integrate the information while avoiding plagiarism.

9. Draw evidence from literary or informational texts to support analysis, reflection, and research.

Range of Writing

10. Write routinely over extended time frames (time for research, reflection, and revision) and shorter time frames (a single sitting or a day or two) for a range of tasks, purposes, and audiences.

Speaking and Listening Standards (6)

Comprehension and Collaboration

1. Prepare for and participate effectively in a range of conversations and collaborations with diverse partners, building on others' ideas and expressing their own clearly and persuasively.

2. Integrate and evaluate information presented in diverse media and formats, including visually, quantitatively, and orally.

3. Evaluate a speaker's point of view, reasoning, and use of evidence and rhetoric.

Presentation of Knowledge and Ideas

4. Present information, findings, and supporting evidence such that listeners can follow the line of reasoning and the organization, development, and style are appropriate to task, purpose, and audience.

2. Then have them think about one thing that their group did really well on their diagram. Then ask them to think about a way they might have done something differently and discuss it in their group.

VI. Assessment

Choice 1

Have each student write down an example of a text feature and two facts about the animal for which their group presented.

Choice 2

Evaluate the groups on their diagram and oral presentation.

 Collaborative Teacher Activity

What's My Home?

I. Materials: animal books, environment books, large manila or poster paper, pencils, crayons, markers, computers if available

II. Instructions

1. Tell the students that they will work in groups to create a way to show a specific environment and three animals that live there by choosing an interesting way to present information about that environment and its representative animals. You may want to have the students choose only two animals. Activities can range from reports to visuals to any technology they choose to use to present their information.

2. They will label features on the animals that show ways those animals are suited to live in that environment.

3. They will also post three to four interesting facts about their environment.

III. Activity

1. Instruct the students to assemble into their groups.

2. Assign the environments to the groups: grasslands, pond, underground, seas or oceans, tide pool, tundra, boreal forest, deciduous forest, rain forest.

3. Review and post their requirements: three animals with labeled features and three to

four facts about their environment or habitat. You may want them to include the title, author, and publisher of the book(s) they used.

4. Provide preselected books for the students to use. Allow time for the students to discuss and locate their books.

5. Allow the students to work on the assignment.

6. Present their information to the class.

7. Lead a discussion about the ways animals fit well into their environments to cover the essential question.

IV. Reflection

1. Have the students state to a partner what they learned.

V. Assessment

Choice 1

Have each student write the name of their habitat and name two animals that live in that environment. Then write an example of how that animal is suited to live there.

Choice 2

Evaluate the student using their presentations.

Extension Activities

1. Introduce simple food chains. Research to find more animals living in each environment. Use some of those animals and have the students create a simple three-organism food chain.

2. Explore more deeply the characteristics of the different environments the groups studied. Create a picture diagram and label the significant features of that environment.

3. Create a picture and written definition to create a glossary using a variety of words from the project posters. Choose the appropriate number of words to include based on your class's abilities.

4. After reading the book, have the students write a short description of the main idea of the book. Use the phrase, "I am a scientist. I know that _____."

5. Make strategic use of digital media and visual displays of data to express information and enhance understanding of presentations.

6. Adapt speech to a variety of contexts and communicative tasks, demonstrating command of formal English when indicated or appropriate.

Language Standards (6)

Conventions of Standard English

1. Demonstrate command of the conventions of standard English grammar and usage when writing or speaking.

2. Demonstrate command of the conventions of standard English capitalization, punctuation, and spelling when writing.

Knowledge of Language

3. Apply knowledge of language to understand how language functions in different contexts, to make effective choices for meaning or style, and to comprehend more fully when reading or listening.

Vocabulary Acquisition and Use

4. Determine or clarify the meaning of unknown and multiple-meaning words and phrases by using context clues, analyzing meaningful word parts,

and consulting general and specialized reference materials, as appropriate.

5. Demonstrate understanding of figurative language, word relationships, and nuances in word meanings.

6. Acquire and use accurately a range of general academic and domain-specific words and phrases sufficient for reading, writing, speaking, and listening at the college and career readiness level; demonstrate independence in gathering vocabulary knowledge when encountering an unknown term important to comprehension or expression.

Mathematical Practices (7)

1. Make sense of problems and persevere in solving them.

2. Reason abstractly and quantitatively.

3. Construct viable arguments and critique the reasoning of others.

4. Model with mathematics.

5. Use appropriate tools strategically.

6. Attend to precision.

7. Look for and make use of structure.

Modifications for Grades 4–5

1. Follow the activity but require more detailed examples of animal adaptations that allow them to fit into their environment.
2. Ask the students to create two or three text features to reflect their information.
3. Make the presentations but also have the students write to report their information using good writing conventions.

Differentiation strategies:

1. Discuss, define, or review pertinent vocabulary and scientific principles of the assignment after reading the book.
2. Use strategic grouping for the activity.
3. Allow the students to select the books from the shelves rather than preselecting them.
4. Require that the students use a variety of resources, such as online information or databases.
5. Let the students choose their own way of presenting the text features and have them incorporate technology in them.
6. Increase the number of animals per environment and show them in a food chain or web relationship in their text features.

Resources:

Biomes
http://www.ucmp.berkeley.edu/glossary/gloss5/biome/

More about biomes
http://kids.nceas.ucsb.edu/biomes/index.html

Interactive introduction to adaptations using bird feet
http://www.vtaide.com/png/bird-adaptations2.htm

Interactive introduction to adaptions using bird beaks
http://www.vtaide.com/png/bird-adaptations3.htm

Explanation of adaptations
http://www.tburg.k12.ny.us/mcdonald/ANIMAL%20ADAPTATIONS/AAdapt.htm

Exemplar Texts:

A Temperate Forest Food Chain: A Who-Eats-What Adventure in North America.
By Rebecca Hogue Wojahn and Donald Wojahn. Lerner, 2009. 64p. (9780822574965)
Grade Level: 3–5
ATOS Reading Level: 5.2
Lexile Level: 790L
Dewey: 577.3

Earth's Biomes.
By Donna Latham. Raintree, 2009. 48p. (9781410933379)
Grade Level: 4–8
ATOS Reading Level: 5.4
Lexile Level: 770L
Dewey: 577

Nature's Patchwork Quilt: Understanding Habitats.
By Mary Miche. Dawn Publications, 2012. 32p. (9781584691709)
Grade Level: K–3
ATOS Reading Level: 4.7
Lexile Level: AD 890L
Dewey: 577

Secrets of the Garden: Food Chains and the Food Web in Our Backyard.
By Kathleen Weidner Zoehfeld. Random, 2012. 40p. (9780517709917)
Grade Level: K–2
ATOS Reading Level: 3.5
Dewey: E

The World of Food Chains with Max Axiom, Super Scientist.
By Liam O'Donnell. Capstone, 2007. 32p. (9781426310393)
Grade Level: 3–9
ATOS Reading Level: 4.9
Lexile Level: GN 720L
Dewey: 577.16

Mathematical Content (6)

Counting and Cardinality
- Count to tell the number of objects.
- Compare numbers.

Operations and Algebraic Thinking
- Analyze patterns and relationships.

Measurement and Data
- Describe and compare measurable attributes.
- Classify objects and count the number of objects in categories.
- Represent and interpret data.

6

Oceans and Seas

By Margaret Hynes. Kingfisher, 2010. 32p. (9780753464151)

Grade Level: 3–5 *(Grades K–2 with modifications)*
Lexile Level: NC 1130L (Non-Conforming)
Dewey: 551.46
Subject Area: science, reading, writing

Essential Question: What allows animals to live in a specific water ecosystem?

Unit Summary: Students will examine the essential question, "What allows animals to live in a specific water ecosystem?" Students will be grouped and assigned a specific ecosystem chosen from the suggested list. They will conduct research using a variety of sources to identify important information about an animal that lives in their assigned ecosystem and identify the adaptations the animal has that allows it to successfully live there. Each group will then select a poem that relates to their ecosystem or animal. The groups will work together to present their information to the class about the animal, the adaptations, and a poem relating to their subject.

Vocabulary: anemone, aphotic, crust, crustaceans, echinoderms, extinct, hurricanes, hydrothermal vents, kelp, migrations, ooze, subduction zones, trench, tsunami, upwelling

Approximate lesson time: two class periods

Booktalk: A science fiction writer named Arthur C. Clarke once wrote, "How inappropriate to call this planet Earth when it is quite clearly ocean." Our Earth is about

Common Core State Standards (50 total)

Reading Standards (7)

Key Ideas and Details

1. Read closely to determine what the text says explicitly and to make logical inferences from it; cite specific textual evidence when writing or speaking to support conclusions drawn from the text.

2. Determine central ideas or themes of a text and analyze their development; summarize the key supporting details and ideas.

Craft and Structure

4. Interpret words and phrases as they are used in a text, including determining technical, connotative, and figurative meanings, and analyze how specific word choices shape meaning or tone.

5. Analyze the structure of texts, including how specific sentences, paragraphs, and larger portions of the text (e.g., a section, chapter, scene, or stanza) relate to each other and the whole.

6. Assess how point of view or purpose shapes the content and style of a text.

Integration of Knowledge and Ideas

7. Integrate and evaluate content presented in diverse media and formats, including visually and quantitatively, as well as in words.

Range of Reading and Level of Text Complexity

10. Read and comprehend complex literary and informational texts independently and proficiently.

Writing Standards (10)

Text Types and Purposes

1. Write arguments to support claims in an analysis of substantive topics or texts, using valid reasoning and relevant and sufficient evidence.

2. Write informative/explanatory texts to examine and convey complex ideas and information clearly and accurately through the effective selection, organization, and analysis of content.

three-quarters ocean, and most of that is saltwater. Oceans contain about 99 percent of all living space on Earth. Oceans and seas are critical to the other life it supports. Water affects Earth and the people on it in a multitude of ways. Let's take a look at the book *Oceans and Seas* to find out more about the oceans and seas around us.

Book Time

1. Share the booktalk for *Oceans and Seas* (above).
2. Tell the students to listen and write down the subject or big ideas topics that relate to the science of oceans and seas.
3. Read pages 6–17 aloud. Include or skip the sidebars as time allows.
4. Have the students share the ideas related to oceans and seas and discuss them. They should come up with topics such as tectonics, motion and energy in waves, tides, and for producing power, coastal and inland erosion, and food chains. Tell them they'll be using some of these ideas in the lessons to come.

 Library Activity

This is the Life! (Ocean, that is)

I. Materials: pencil and paper, reference books and materials, poetry books about animals and marine habitats, resource materials, computers, graphic organizer

II. Instructions
1. Divide the class into groups of three or four students each.
2. Tell the groups that they will use different kinds of resources to locate information about a specific animal and its habitat and why that animal is suited or adapted to live in its habitat and write it down on the graphic organizer. They will keep a list of their sources. Identify which sources are available to them in your library.
3. They will then choose or be assigned an ecosystem and choose an animal from one of the ecosystems.
4. After they've learned some information about why their animal can live success-

fully in that ecosystem, they must find a poem that relates in some way to their information. It can be about the animal or the ecosystem or address some aspect of their chosen life form.

5. They will select and present the top five facts about their animals from their list and state the adaptations it has to live in that marine ecosystem, and then they will present their poem. The presentations can be oral, written, or done using a form of technology available in your library.

III. Procedure

1. Assign or have the student groups choose one of the following ocean ecosystems: coasts (p. 14), rockpool or tidepool (p. 16), salt marsh/ delta (p. 18), coral reef (p. 20), kelp forest (p. 5), dark zone (also known as aphotic zone, p. 22).

2. Have each group research to find out more about the animal and take notes. Remind them to list their sources. Both of these will be written on the graphic organizer.

3. Find and select a poem relating to their topic and practice reading it. They may do it together or assign individual lines. Remind them you'll be looking for fluency and expression as they read.

🖉 *Suggested lesson break.*

4. Allow time for the research and for student groups to find a poem.

5. Conduct the group presentations.

6. Discuss their findings as a group and relate them to the essential question.

IV. Reflect

1. Ask the students to think over their presentation and write one thing that their group did really well. Then ask them to write something that might have been improved if they did the activity again.

2. Then ask them to rate their poetry reading on a scale of one to ten, with ten being the best they could have done. Have them think about how they might improve the reading if they did it again.

3. Write narratives to develop real or imagined experiences or events using effective technique, well-chosen details, and well-structured event sequences.

Production and Distribution of Writing

4. Produce clear and coherent writing in which the development, organization, and style are appropriate to task, purpose, and audience.

5. Develop and strengthen writing as needed by planning, revising, editing, rewriting, or trying a new approach.

6. Use technology, including the Internet, to produce and publish writing and to interact and collaborate with others.

Research to Build and Present Knowledge

7. Conduct short as well as more sustained research projects based on focused questions, demonstrating understanding of the subject under investigation.

8. Gather relevant information from multiple print and digital sources, assess the credibility and accuracy of each source, and integrate the information while avoiding plagiarism.

9. Draw evidence from literary or informational

texts to support analysis, reflection, and research.

Range of Writing

10. Write routinely over extended time frames (time for research, reflection, and revision) and shorter time frames (a single sitting or a day or two) for a range of tasks, purposes, and audiences.

Speaking and Listening Standards (6)

Comprehension and Collaboration

1. Prepare for and participate effectively in a range of conversations and collaborations with diverse partners, building on others' ideas and expressing their own clearly and persuasively.

2. Integrate and evaluate information presented in diverse media and formats, including visually, quantitatively, and orally.

3. Evaluate a speaker's point of view, reasoning, and use of evidence and rhetoric.

Presentation of Knowledge and Ideas

4. Present information, findings, and supporting evidence such that listeners can follow the line of reasoning and the organization, development, and style are appropriate to

VI. Assessment

Choice 1

Have each student summarize the information they learned by writing a short paragraph about their information without using their notes.

Choice 2

Evaluate the groups on their presentation and poetry reading.

 Collaborative Teacher Activity

Energy in the Ocean

I. Materials: poster board; map; pencils and markers; copy of the book; additional books about: tectonic movement, ocean motion and waves, tidal power, wind power, coastal and inland erosion, and food chains; list from library of related topics from discussion

II. Instructions

1. Tell the students that they will work in groups to create a visual with labels to illustrate the different forms of energy related to oceans and seas. Review the list of topics they noticed from the library lesson and add to the list to include tectonic motion; wave energy; tidal, wind, and wave electricity production; erosion; and food chains.

2. Assign the students to one of four groups. Each group will work together to create a visual. They will also generate a list of at least five vocabulary words with their definitions that relate to the topic. Use these four topics (and any others generated by the students that do not fall into these categories, and add another group): (1) tectonic motion; (2) energy of waves and significance, including ocean-generated power (wind, wave, and tidal); (3) erosion and resulting impact; (4) food chains.

3. Let students know that their visuals will be modeled on a spread in the book. Review several spreads and discuss the text and graphic features that present the information. Then show them a spread and point

out the design and placement of information, including a representative website.

III. Activity

1. Instruct the students to assemble into their groups. Tell them they need to listen and note all parts of their topic.
2. Return to the book and read pages 6–17 again.
3. Tell the students they must turn in a planned design for their visuals before beginning. They will also turn in a vocabulary list with the meanings on it before the group works on their presentation visual.
4. Have the students begin reading and noting ideas for planning their poster and vocabulary.
5. Allow enough time for all groups to complete the assignment.

Suggested lesson break.

6. Present the vocabulary and visuals.
7. Ask the students listening to each presentation to write down three to five important points made by the group during the presentation.

IV. Reflection

1. After the presentations, have the students review their visual and have each person in the group tell something they liked about their presentation and something they might have done better.

V. Assessment

Choice 1

List the topics and instruct the students to write a brief summary of the information they learned about each topic. Let them refer to their notes, if you wish. You can leave the posters in place or cover or remove them.

Choice 2

Select two vocabulary words from each topic and ask the students to write about and explain them.

Extension Activities

1. Investigate James Cook and other early ocean explorers. Create a timeline of the early

task, purpose, and audience.

5. Make strategic use of digital media and visual displays of data to express information and enhance understanding of presentations.

6. Adapt speech to a variety of contexts and communicative tasks, demonstrating command of formal English when indicated or appropriate.

Language Standards (6)

Conventions of Standard English

1. Demonstrate command of the conventions of standard English grammar and usage when writing or speaking.

2. Demonstrate command of the conventions of standard English capitalization, punctuation, and spelling when writing.

Knowledge of Language

3. Apply knowledge of language to understand how language functions in different contexts, to make effective choices for meaning or style, and to comprehend more fully when reading or listening.

Vocabulary Acquisition and Use

4. Determine or clarify the meaning of unknown and multiple-meaning words

and phrases by using context clues, analyzing meaningful word parts, and consulting general and specialized reference materials, as appropriate.

5. Demonstrate understanding of figurative language, word relationships, and nuances in word meanings.

6. Acquire and use accurately a range of general academic and domain-specific words and phrases sufficient for reading, writing, speaking, and listening at the college and career readiness level; demonstrate independence in gathering vocabulary knowledge when encountering an unknown term important to comprehension or expression.

Mathematical Practices (7)

1. Make sense of problems and persevere in solving them.

2. Reason abstractly and quantitatively.

3. Construct viable arguments and critique the reasoning of others.

4. Model with mathematics.

5. Use appropriate tools strategically.

6. Attend to precision.

explorations and where they took place from journey's start to end. Add information about the explorers.
2. Look up cultured pearls and read about the process for creating these pearls. Write a description of how it's done and the science behind it.
3. Explore the issues facing oceans today. Name the largest issues and assign students to research and present the information in a debate-style setting.
4. After reading the book, have the students write a short description of the main idea of the book. Use the phrase, "I am a scientist. I know that _____."

Modifications for Grades K–2

1. Use the book to identify the various ecosystems and write the names where everyone can see them. Assign the groups to one of the ecosystems (coastline, intertidal pool, salt marsh/delta, coral reef, kelp forest, dark zone (also known as aphotic zone).
2. Have the groups of students find information about their assigned ecosystem using books that you have made available.
3. Each group will identify an animal that lives in their ecosystem and find three important facts about it.
4. Illustrate a visual and post their facts, and then present them to the class.

Differentiation strategies:

1. Preselect the books and reference materials you want the students to use.
2. Discuss, define, or review the vocabulary before or after reading the book. Point out examples of how the words were used in the book.
3. Use strategic grouping for the activity.
4. Allow students to present their information in other ways, including through the use of technology.
5. Have the students work individually.

6. Eliminate the poem requirement or challenge the students to write their own original poem using the information they learned from their research.

7. Increase the amount of information they must put on their visuals and ask them to write about it rather than listing the facts.

Resources:

Site with general information specific to California
http://resources.ca.gov/ocean/html/chapt_4.html

General current information and good images
http://ocean.si.edu/ocean-life-ecosystems

General information about the ocean
http://ocean.nationalgeographic.com/ocean/

NOAA's site for kids has an activity book with resources listed on various pages
http://oceanservice.noaa.gov/education/welcome.html

Exemplar Texts:

Ocean.
By Miranda MacQuitty. DK Pub., 2008. 72p. (9780756637767)
Grade Level: 4–8
ATOS Reading Level: 7.7
Lexile Level: IG 1180L
Dewey: 551.46

Oceans.
By Peter Benoit. Children's Press, 2011. 48p. (9780531205563)
Grade Level: K–3
ATOS Reading Level: 5.8
Lexile Level: 930L
Dewey: 551.46

Oceans. (Ripley's Believe It or Not!)
By Camilla de la Bedoyere. Mason Crest, 2011. 48p. (9781893951815)
Grade Level: 4–7
Lexile Level: IG 1060L
Dewey: 551.46

7. Look for and make use of structure.

Mathematical Content (14)

Counting and Cardinality
- Know number names and the count sequence.
- Count to tell the number of objects.
- Compare numbers.

Operations and Algebraic Thinking
- Write and interpret numerical expressions.
- Analyze patterns and relationships.

Number and Operations in Base Ten
- Generalize place value understanding for multi-digit whole numbers.

Measurement and Data
- Describe and compare measurable attributes.
- Classify objects and count the number of objects in categories.
- Measure and estimate lengths in standard units.
- Tell and write time.
- Solve problems involving measurement and estimation of intervals of time, liquid volumes, and masses of objects.
- Perform operations with multi-digit whole numbers and with decimals to hundredths.
- Convert like measurement units within a

given measurement system.
• Represent and interpret data.

Oceans: Dolphins, Sharks, Penguins, and More! Meet 60 Cool Sea Creatures and Explore their Amazing Watery World
By Johnna Rizzo. National Geographic, 2010. 64p. (9781426306860)
Grade Level: 4–8
ATOS Reading Level: 7.2
Dewey: 578.77

Ocean Sunlight: How Tiny Plants Feed the Seas.
By Molly Bang and Penny Chisholm. Scholastic/Blue Sky, 2012. 48p. (9780545273220)
Grade Level: K–3
ATOS Reading Level: 4.5
Lexile Level: 770L
Dewey: 571.4

7 Planting the Wild Garden

By Kathryn O. Galbraith. Peachtree, 2011. 32p. (9781561455638)

Grade Level: 1–3 *(Modifications for Grade K and Grades 4–5)*
ATOS Reading Level: 2.0
Lexile Level: AD 490L (Adult Directed)
Dewey: 581.467
Subject Area: science, language arts

Essential Question: How are seeds spread to different places?

Unit Summary: Students will examine the essential question, "How are seeds spread to different places?" They will listen as you read the book and notice the different ways seeds are spread. Together, the class will create a chart to name the different ways seeds are spread. From this chart, students will work with a graphic organizer that develops the concept and helps them remember how seeds are spread in nature.

Vocabulary: acorn, amble, cockleburs, droppings, fields, garden, goldfinches, hitchhike, lodge, masked, meadow, minnows, nibble, oval, patters, prickly, shadow, splatter, stream, strewn, thistles

Approximate lesson time: one to two class periods

Booktalk: You might have planted seeds before. But many times, seeds grow in places where people didn't plant them. Where did they come from? Science helps us

Common Core State Standards (55 total)

Reading Standards (7)

Key Ideas and Details

1. Read closely to determine what the text says explicitly and to make logical inferences from it; cite specific textual evidence when writing or speaking to support conclusions drawn from the text.

2. Determine central ideas or themes of a text and analyze their development; summarize the key supporting details and ideas.

3. Analyze how and why individuals, events, and ideas develop and interact over the course of a text.

Craft and Structure

4. Interpret words and phrases as they are used in a text, including determining technical, connotative, and figurative meanings, and analyze how specific word choices shape meaning or tone.

Integration of Knowledge and Ideas

7. Integrate and evaluate content presented in diverse media and formats, including visually and quantitatively, as well as in words.

8. Delineate and evaluate the argument and specific claims in a text, including the validity of the reasoning as well as the relevance and sufficiency of the evidence.

Range of Reading and Level of Text Complexity

10. Read and comprehend complex literary and informational texts independently and proficiently.

Writing Standards (8)

Text Types and Purposes

1. Write arguments to support claims in an analysis of substantive topics or texts, using valid reasoning and relevant and sufficient evidence.

2. Write informative/explanatory texts to examine and convey complex ideas and information clearly and accu-

find out. How can science help us learn how plants get in the place where they grow? Let's take a look at the book *Planting the Wild Garden* to find out.

Book Time

1. Ask the students to talk about their experiences in planting seeds. Discuss what seeds need to grow and what the students did to help their seeds grow.
2. Ask the students the meaning of "meadow." Show images of meadows or places wild plants might be and discuss how the plants got there.
3. Share the booktalk for *Planting the Wild Garden* (above).
4. Tell the students you are going to read the book to them.
5. Ask them to look for different ways that seeds get planted as they listen to the book.
6. Read the book aloud. You may need to stop and clarify the vocabulary in the book as you read. For example, the sentence, "Waves of black and gold dip into the meadow" may require further explanation or discussion.
7. Use the rich art in this book to further develop the appreciation of picture books and help explain the text.
8. After reading, lead a discussion with the students about the different ways seeds are spread. Examples from the book include: wind, rain, streams, sun, sticking to rabbit fur and raccoon fur, squirrels bury acorns, muddy boots, seeds stick to clothing (sweaters and socks), people blow on seeds.
9. List the ways students remember that seeds were spread using a word or two on a chart. Prompt them to add the remaining ways by reviewing the pages in the book to complete the list. After each way is listed, have the students think of a way to show the word kinesthetically. Practice acting out the method of spreading for each way.

Most of these words should be listed: wind, rain, streams, sun, rabbits eating, rabbit fur, raccoon fur, squirrels bury acorns, muddy boots, seeds stick to clothing (sweaters and socks), people blow on seeds.

✐ *Suggested lesson break*.

 Library Activity

Spreading Seeds in Nature

I.   Materials: sheets of blank paper, crayons or map pencils, graphic organizer
II. Instructions
   1. Tell the students they will be using a graphic organizer to show the different ways seeds are spread. If necessary, read the book again to review the ways seeds are spread.
   2. Hand out the printed graphic organizer and have them get out crayons or map pencils.
III. Procedure
   1. Have the students find the center circle. Tell them to write the word *seed* in it.
   2. Remind them they are filling out a graphic organizer to help them remember all the ways seeds travel.
   3. Point to the chart where "rain" is listed. Tell them to write *rain* in one of the circles and add an arrow to show that seeds are spread by rain.
   4. Have them write another way seeds are spread in a different circle on the graphic organizer.
   5. Tell them they will continue to add the different ways seeds are spread to their graphic organizer by adding more words. Continue adding the arrows from the "seed" circle to each circle they add. Continue to model as needed for your group.
   7. Illustrate each word in the graphic organizer.
   8. On the back of their paper, have the students draw a picture of their favorite way seeds travel in the wild and write a sentence about it.
   9. Return to the essential question and discuss their findings.

rately through the effective selection, organization, and analysis of content.

Production and Distribution of Writing
4. Produce clear and coherent writing in which the development, organization, and style are appropriate to task, purpose, and audience.

5. Develop and strengthen writing as needed by planning, revising, editing, rewriting, or trying a new approach.

Research to Build and Present Knowledge
7. Conduct short as well as more sustained research projects based on focused questions, demonstrating understanding of the subject under investigation.

8. Gather relevant information from multiple print and digital sources, assess the credibility and accuracy of each source, and integrate the information while avoiding plagiarism.

9. Draw evidence from literary or informational texts to support analysis, reflection, and research.

Range of Writing
10. Write routinely over extended time frames (time for research, reflection, and revision) and shorter time frames (a single sitting or a day or

two) for a range of tasks, purposes, and audiences.

Speaking and Listening Standards (5)

Comprehension and Collaboration

1. Prepare for and participate effectively in a range of conversations and collaborations with diverse partners, building on others' ideas and expressing their own clearly and persuasively.

2. Integrate and evaluate information presented in diverse media and formats, including visually, quantitatively, and orally.

Presentation of Knowledge and Ideas

4. Present information, findings, and supporting evidence such that listeners can follow the line of reasoning and the organization, development, and style are appropriate to task, purpose, and audience.

5. Make strategic use of digital media and visual displays of data to express information and enhance understanding of presentations.

6. Adapt speech to a variety of contexts and communicative tasks, demonstrating command of formal English when indicated or appropriate.

IV.   Reflect
1. Ask the students to turn to the person next to them and read the graphic organizer circles to one another.
2. Then have them silently look at their paper. Ask them to think about another way a seed might be spread. Add that idea to the graphic organizer.
3. After a few minutes, have students who thought of other ways seeds are spread to share their ideas. Give time for all students to add at least one more way. Answers might include other animals, cars, boats, fish, airplanes, or any other answer that can be reasonably defended. Discuss their answers.

VI.   Assessment

Choice 1

Post this list: who, what, where, when, why, and how

Tell the students they will write a question and its answer about the ways seeds move in nature. Have the students choose from three to six of the question words. Using their graphic organizer, have them write a question for each of the words they chose. They must use the chosen word in their question. Then they will write the answer to their question in a complete sentence. They may use examples they remember from the book, their graphic organizer, or another one that comes to mind.

Choice 2

On the back of their papers, have the students write the title, "Seeds Travel By?" Ask them to number one, two, and three, leaving enough space to write under each number. Have the students list three ways seeds travel and draw a picture to accompany it without looking back at their graphic organizer.

 Collaborative Teacher Activity

Living or Nonliving Pictograph

I.   Materials: paper for a pictograph, map pencils

II. Instructions
1. Review the difference between living and nonliving things. Living is anything that is alive or was before. It can be dead, like a tree trunk, but was formerly alive. Examples may include flowers, people, pets, trees, and logs. Nonliving includes anything that has never been alive or will be. It may move, but motion doesn't mean alive. Examples include glass, water, wind, and rocks.
2. Go back through the book and discuss the text and pictures. Identify the living and nonliving elements named.
3. Make a list of all the living and nonliving things in the order introduced in the book. Post it where everyone can see.
4. Tell the students they are going to make a pictograph of the living and nonliving things from *Planting the Wild Garden.*

III. Activity
1. Review what a pictograph is like. Discuss symbols for the list of living and nonliving chart words. Put the symbols next to the words on the chart.
2. Instruct the students to title their paper "Planting the Wild Garden."
3. Have them make two columns. Title one "Living" and the other one "Nonliving."
4. Tell them to create their pictographs using the symbols from their list by placing each thing into the correct category.
5. For older grades, have the students next add gardening-related words of their own that are examples of living and nonliving things in nature. You might provide some examples, such as minerals, water, rocks, etc. Then ask them to write about another way they might show examples of living and nonliving things.

IV. Reflection
1. Have the students place their completed pictographs on their desks.
2. Tell them to walk around the room and look at the other pictographs without talking.

Language Standards (6)

Conventions of Standard English

1. Demonstrate command of the conventions of standard English grammar and usage when writing or speaking.

2. Demonstrate command of the conventions of standard English capitalization, punctuation, and spelling when writing.

Knowledge of Language

3. Apply knowledge of language to understand how language functions in different contexts, to make effective choices for meaning or style, and to comprehend more fully when reading or listening.

Vocabulary Acquisition and Use

4. Determine or clarify the meaning of unknown and multiple-meaning words and phrases by using context clues, analyzing meaningful word parts, and consulting general and specialized reference materials, as appropriate.

5. Demonstrate understanding of figurative language, word relationships, and nuances in word meanings.

6. Acquire and use accurately a range of general academic and domain-specific words and phrases

sufficient for reading, writing, speaking, and listening at the college and career readiness level; demonstrate independence in gathering vocabulary knowledge when encountering an unknown term important to comprehension or expression.

Mathematical Practices (7)

1. Make sense of problems and persevere in solving them.

2. Reason abstractly and quantitatively.

3. Construct viable arguments and critique the reasoning of others.

4. Model with mathematics.

5. Use appropriate tools strategically.

6. Attend to precision.

7. Look for and make use of structure.

Mathematical Content (22)

Counting and Cardinality
- Know number names and the count sequence.
- Count to tell the number of objects.
- Compare numbers.

Operations and Algebraic Thinking
- Represent and solve problems involving

3. When they return to their desks, have them review their own graphs. Ask them to add one more thing to each column, but this time use something that is not from the book.

V. Assessment

Choice 1

Remove the class chart and pick up the students' pictographs. Have the students make a new chart for living and nonliving things. Then tell them to put three things from the book into each column using words or pictures. Alternatively, have them write to explain some of the living and nonliving components in nature and the part they play in spreading seeds.

Choice 2

Draw a picture and/or write words on a sticky note to show one living thing and one nonliving thing. Students place their sticky notes on the graphic organizer chart titled Living/Nonliving. Discuss the choices with the class.

Extension Activities

1. Plant corn seeds and bean seeds. Observe their growth as they sprout and measure the size each day. Make a line graph to illustrate their growth over three weeks.
2. After reading the book, have the students write a short description of the main idea of the book *Planting the Wild Garden.* Use the phrase, "I am a scientist. I know that _____."
3. Have the students bring in seeds they can find at home and around their homes. Group the seeds into wild seeds and seeds that people plant. Display the seeds.

Modifications for Grade K

1. After reading the book, return to the beginning and as you come across a way seeds are spread, stop and have the students fill it in on their graphic organizer.

2. Continue through the book, making sure the students understand how the seeds are spread.
3. Then have them illustrate each method and write words to identify something in their pictures.
4. Have the students write one to three sentences on the back of their papers to explain a few ways seeds are spread.

Modifications for Grades 4–5

1. Identify the ways seeds are spread as you read the book and have the students list them.
2. In groups, ask the students to find examples of specific seeds that are spread in each category they named.
3. Choose one seed species and have them extend their research to create a visual of that plant's life cycle.
4. Next have the groups find where the seed grows to add to their visual display or include it on a map.

Differentiation strategies:

1. Discuss, define, or review the vocabulary after reading the book.
2. Allow the students to develop their own graphic organizer.
3. Create the illustrations in a 3-dimensional art form.
4. Use strategic grouping by working in pairs or small groups.
5. Model the final product before the students do the work.
6. Allow students to present their graphic organizers in other formats.

Resources:

Plant dispersal
http://www.brainpopjr.com/science/plants/plantlife
   cycle/grownups.weml

Living and nonliving
http://glencoe.mcgraw-hill.com/sites/dl/
   free/0078617022/167348/00076707.html

addition and subtraction.
- Understand and apply properties of operations and the relationship between addition and subtraction.
- Work with addition and subtraction equations.
- Work with equal groups of objects to gain foundations for multiplication.
- Generate and analyze patterns.
- Write and interpret numerical expressions.
- Analyze patterns and relationships.

Number and Operations in Base Ten
- Use place value understanding and properties of operations to perform multi-digit arithmetic.

Measurement and Data
- Describe and compare measurable attributes.
- Classify objects and count the number of objects in categories.
- Measure lengths indirectly and by iterating length units.
- Tell and write time.
- Measure and estimate lengths in standard units.
- Relate addition and subtraction to length.
- Solve problems involving measurement and estimation of intervals of time, liquid volumes, and masses of objects.

- Solve problems involving measurement and conversion of measurements from a larger unit to a smaller unit.
- Convert like measurement units within a given measurement system.
- Represent and interpret data.

Geometry
- Graph points on the coordinate plane to solve real-world and mathematical problems.

Conditions for seed dispersal
http://theseedsite.co.uk/dispersal.html

Kid-friendly information about spreading seeds
http://library.thinkquest.org/3715/seeds4.html

Exemplar Texts:

A Seed Is Sleepy.
By Dianna Hutts Aston. Chronicle Books, 2007. 40p.
(9780811855204)
Grade Level: 1–4
ATOS Reading Level: 3.8
Lexile Level: AD 750L
Dewey: 581.467

From Seed to Plant.
By Allan Fowler. Childrens Press, 2001. 32p.
   (9780516273075)
Grade Level: K–3.
ATOS Reading Level: 2.3
Dewey: 581.467

Seeds.
By Ken Robbins. Atheneum, 2005. 32p. (9780689850417)
Grade Level: PreS–3
ATOS Reading Level: 4.4
Dewey: 582.046

Seeds Go, Seeds Grow.
By Mark Weakland. Capstone Press, 2011. 32p. (9781429652520)
Grade Level: PreK–2
ATOS Reading Level: 2.7
Lexile Level: NC 710L
Dewey: 581.4

Sunflowers.
By Julie K. Lundgren. Rourke, 2011. 24p. (9781615903078)
Grade Level: 1–4
ATOS Reading Level: 4.2
Dewey: 635.9

8
Rocks and Minerals

By Steve Tomecek. National Geographic, 2010. 32p. (0781426305382)

Grade Level: 3–5 *(Grades K–2 with modifications)*
ATOS Reading Level: 5.2
Lexile Level: NC 860L (Non-Conforming)
Dewey: 552
Subject Area: science, language arts

Essential Question: What are rocks made of?

Unit Summary: Students will examine the essential question, "What are rocks made of?" They will listen to selected portions of the book and refer back to specific book sections to answer questions about the basic kinds of rock formation as a large group. They will then work collaboratively in groups to identify vocabulary and collect pertinent research information about their rock group. The groups will prepare a poster to convey the information and then exchange vocabulary definitions with the other groups. Groups will also present their poster information while the other groups take notes on a graphic organizer.

Vocabulary: basalt, crust, crystals, deposit, erosion, flow, folds, gabbro, gneiss, granite, heated, ice, igneous, lava, layers, limestone, magma, metamorphic, mountains, schist, sediment, sedimentary, squeezed, tectonic plates, water, weathering, wind, volcanoes,

Approximate lesson time: two to four class periods

Common Core State Standards (51 total)

Reading Standards (6)

Key Ideas and Details

1. Read closely to determine what the text says explicitly and to make logical inferences from it; cite specific textual evidence when writing or speaking to support conclusions drawn from the text.

2. Determine central ideas or themes of a text and analyze their development; summarize the key supporting details and ideas.

Craft and Structure

4. Interpret words and phrases as they are used in a text, including determining technical, connotative, and figurative meanings, and analyze how specific

word choices shape meaning or tone.

Integration of Knowledge and Ideas

7. Integrate and evaluate content presented in diverse media and formats, including visually and quantitatively, as well as in words.

8. Delineate and evaluate the argument and specific claims in a text, including the validity of the reasoning as well as the relevance and sufficiency of the evidence.

Range of Reading and Level of Text Complexity

10. Read and comprehend complex literary and informational texts independently and proficiently.

Writing Standards (9)

Text Types and Purposes

2. Write informative/ explanatory texts to examine and convey complex ideas and information clearly and accurately through the effective selection, organization, and analysis of content.

3. Write narratives to develop real or imagined experiences or events using effective technique, well-chosen details, and well-structured event sequences.

Booktalk: Look closely at a ring or necklace made with stones. These stones are gems, and they're formed of minerals. Minerals make up most rocks. But not all rocks are gems. You've probably picked up a rock and examined it. What did you notice? Was it dark, or did it have colors? Were there tiny pieces inside it? Was it smooth or rough? Did it crumble in your hand? Let's find out how rocks are formed. We'll take a look at the book *Rocks and Minerals* to find out.

Book Time

1. Share the booktalk for *Rocks and Minerals* (above).
2. Ask students what a geologist does. Take answers, and make sure they include the fact that a geologist is a scientist who studies rocks.
3. Tell the students you are going to read the first part of the book to them.
4. Ask them to listen for the layers of the Earth, what rocks are made of, and how rocks are used.
5. Read pages 5–13 aloud.
6. Review with the students the Earth's layers (inner and outer core, mantle, and crust; p. 7), what rocks are made of (minerals, many of which form crystals; p. 8–9), and how rocks are used (tools, weapons, buildings, etc.; p. 10–11). Ask the students to tell what helped them remember the section where the answer is found.
7. Ask the students if they know the names of the three kinds of rocks. Take answers and post the words igneous, metamorphic, and sedimentary where everyone can see them. Tell them they will be learning about how each of these kinds of rocks form.
8. Pass out the graphic organizer and fill in the information they remember from the reading. Tell them to skip ones they don't remember, but remind them to discuss it with someone else before skipping it. You may do this in groups or individually. Then go through each number on the graphic organizer and review the answers by locating them in the book. Give all students the opportunity to fill in any missing answers.

✎ Suggested lesson break.

 Library Activity

How Are Rocks Formed?

I. Materials: other books about rock formation, reference books, computer access, poster board or large paper (or whiteboard), printed list of vocabulary words, graphic organizer

II. Instructions
1. Divide the class into three groups (if it's a large class, you may want to have six groups). Assign each group one of the topics: igneous, metamorphic, or sedimentary.
2. Tell the groups that they will use different resources to answer the question about how rocks are formed for their topic. They will keep a list of their sources. For grade 3, you may want to select the resources they will use.
3. They will present their information to the class and write notes about the rock formation from the other groups.

III. Procedure
1. Give each group one of the following words relating to their topic to guide them in their research: igneous, metamorphic, or sedimentary. Use the vocabulary listed below for the lesson. They will need to include these words in their fact list. Tell them to divide up the words and then later share their information with the other group members so everyone has the meanings. They will later add the meanings to the words from each of the other groups. You can use the books from your library and the URLs that follow the lesson.

Provide a list of words after each kind of rock to the students to use for the activity:
   a. igneous: magma, crystals, granite, gabbro, lava, volcanoes, basalt, crust
   b. metamorphic: heated, squeezed, flow, gneiss, schist, tectonic plates, mountains, folds

Production and Distribution of Writing

4. Produce clear and coherent writing in which the development, organization, and style are appropriate to task, purpose, and audience.

5. Develop and strengthen writing as needed by planning, revising, editing, rewriting, or trying a new approach.

6. Use technology, including the Internet, to produce and publish writing and to interact and collaborate with others.

Research to Build and Present Knowledge

7. Conduct short as well as more sustained research projects based on focused questions, demonstrating understanding of the subject under investigation.

8. Gather relevant information from multiple print and digital sources, assess the credibility and accuracy of each source, and integrate the information while avoiding plagiarism.

9. Draw evidence from literary or informational texts to support analysis, reflection, and research.

Range of Writing

10. Write routinely over extended time frames (time for research, reflection, and revision) and

Speaking and Listening Standards (6)

Comprehension and Collaboration

1. Prepare for and participate effectively in a range of conversations and collaborations with diverse partners, building on others' ideas and expressing their own clearly and persuasively.

2. Integrate and evaluate information presented in diverse media and formats, including visually, quantitatively, and orally.

3. Evaluate a speaker's point of view, reasoning, and use of evidence and rhetoric.

Presentation of Knowledge and Ideas

4. Present information, findings, and supporting evidence such that listeners can follow the line of reasoning and the organization, development, and style are appropriate to task, purpose, and audience.

5. Make strategic use of digital media and visual displays of data to express information and enhance understanding of presentations.

shorter time frames (a single sitting or a day or two) for a range of tasks, purposes, and audiences.

---

c. sedimentary: sediment, wind, water, ice, weathering, erosion, deposit, layers, limestone

For grade 3, you may want to preprint the definitions or set aside an additional period for vocabulary presentations.

2. Each group will conduct short research to identify pertinent facts about their group's topic of rock formation.

3. Each student writes a list of important facts relating to their topic. The group will work together and share facts. They will keep this list to use for the poster. Remind them to save their individual lists.

✐ *Suggested lesson break.*

4. Each group then will make a large poster of their information. Remind them to write large enough for everyone to see. At the bottom or on the back, list their resources.

5. When the students finish their research, one person in each of the groups will read the related pages from the book *Rocks and Minerals* to their group members.

6. Pass out the graphic organizer chart labeled with igneous, metamorphic, and sedimentary.

7. One at a time, each group will present their poster of information. Each student will write three important facts about each topic from the presentations.

✐ *Suggested lesson break.*

8. Have each group present their vocabulary. The students may create their own method of presenting the words so that everyone can see the meanings. This may involve typing and printing them, oral presentations, posting them on the posters, presenting them using technology, or having students moving throughout the room to collect them in pairs from other groups.

9. Lead a short wrap-up discussion to answer the essential question.

10. Tell the students to keep their lists to use in the classroom.

IV. Reflect

1. Have the students silently read their list of facts they included on the poster. Then have them find a fact from the poster of the other two groups that reminds them of a similarity or difference in their kind of rock formation.

VI. Assessment

Choice 1

Have each student summarize the information they learned by writing a short paragraph about their information. Remind them to use the correct form.

Choice 2

Ask each student to explain three words related to their topic of rock formation.

 Collaborative Teacher Activity

The Rock Cycle

I. Materials: posters from library activity, map pencils; blank paper, list of vocabulary words

II. Instructions

1. Tell the students that they will be creating a graphic image with labels that illustrates the stages of the rock cycle. Review the posters created in the library lesson.

2. Go back through the book and read pages 26 and 27. After reading, review in more detail how the rock cycle works.

3. Hand out a list of the vocabulary. Review the words to make sure the students understand them.

Vocabulary for collaborative lesson: changing, deposits, erosion, folding, ice, igneous rocks, magma, melting, metamorphic rocks, pressure, rain, sedimentary rocks, sediments, squeezing, volcano, water, weathering, wind

4. They will work in groups to diagram the rock cycle using the words and drawings to help illustrate it.

6. Adapt speech to a variety of contexts and communicative tasks, demonstrating command of formal English when indicated or appropriate.

Language Standards (5)

Conventions of Standard English

1. Demonstrate command of the conventions of standard English grammar and usage when writing or speaking.

2. Demonstrate command of the conventions of standard English capitalization, punctuation, and spelling when writing.

Knowledge of Language

3. Apply knowledge of language to understand how language functions in different contexts, to make effective choices for meaning or style, and to comprehend more fully when reading or listening.

Vocabulary Acquisition and Use

4. Determine or clarify the meaning of unknown and multiple-meaning words and phrases by using context clues, analyzing meaningful word parts, and consulting general and specialized reference materials, as appropriate.

6. Acquire and use accurately a range of general academic and domain-

specific words and phrases sufficient for reading, writing, speaking, and listening at the college and career readiness level; demonstrate independence in gathering vocabulary knowledge when encountering an unknown term important to comprehension or expression.

Mathematical Practices (7)

1. Make sense of problems and persevere in solving them.

2. Reason abstractly and quantitatively.

3. Construct viable arguments and critique the reasoning of others.

4. Model with mathematics.

5. Use appropriate tools strategically.

6. Attend to precision.

7. Look for and make use of structure.

Mathematical Content (18)

Counting and Cardinality

- Know number names and the count sequence.
- Count to tell the number of objects.
- Compare numbers.

5. Then they will write to explain the rock cycle.

6. Review the meaning of the rock cycle. Rock formation begins at one point and over long amounts of time returns to the point where it started.

III.   Activity

1. Tell the students they will be making and labeling a diagram of the rock cycle in groups.

2. Then they will write to explain the rock cycle using what they learned from the library activity and their rock cycle diagrams.

3. Allow the students time to make their diagrams and write the explanation.

IV.   Reflection

1. Have the students exchange papers and read the paper of another student.

2. Return the papers and instruct them to read their own paper again. Make any changes they wish.

V.   Assessment

Choice 1

Create a chart to compare and contrast the different ways rocks are formed on Earth.

Choice 2

Write a summary of the book *Rocks and Minerals.* Include details that support the summary.

Extension Activities

1. Look up the Mohs hardness test. Then find a picture of each of the minerals listed on the scale. Prepare a document that includes a picture and description of each of the ten minerals.

2. Look up your state mineral. Investigate it, and then find out the state minerals for nearby states.

3. Search for a guide online or in a book that helps you identify minerals. Find three rocks from your area and try to identify them. Start a class collection and work together to name the kinds of rocks you collect.

4. After reading the book, have the students write a short description of the main idea of the book. Use the phrase, "I am a scientist. I know that _____."

Modifications for Grades K–2

1. Read the book's introduction and then talk about the three kinds of rocks in terms of fire-formed (igneous), pressed in layers (sedimentary), and changed under great heat and pressure (metamorphic).
2. Have the students use the graphic organizer and label each science term with the easier words so both will be on the page (igneous = fire-formed; metamorphic = changed by heat or pressure; sedimentary = pressed layers).
3. Read about igneous rocks and have the students draw a volcano to help them remember.
4. Continue to the sedimentary section and have them draw a layer and add more and more layers. Include shells or bones in the image at the bottom that would form fossils.
5. Then draw layers that have pushed upward in a swirl pattern after reading the metamorphic rock section.
6. Have the students write a sentence about each kind of rock type.

Differentiation strategies:

1. Discuss, define, or review the vocabulary before or after reading the book. Point out examples of how the words were used in the book.
2. Identify or list the links that are available to help them locate their rock information.
3. Encourage the students to ask questions during the presentations or to take notes in pairs to support slower writers.
4. Prepare questions to direct the research ahead of time and give them to the students.
5. Read the book a second time. Stop and guide the students as they take notes for the discussion.

Operations and Algebraic Thinking

- Solve problems involving the four operations, and identify and explain patterns in arithmetic.
- Write and interpret numerical expressions.
- Analyze patterns and relationships.

Number and Operations in Base Ten

- Generalize place value understanding for multidigit whole numbers.
- Use place value understanding and properties of operations to perform multi-digit arithmetic.

Measurement and Data

- Describe and compare measurable attributes.
- Classify objects and count the number of objects in categories.
- Tell and write time.
- Solve problems involving measurement and estimation of intervals of time, liquid volumes, and masses of objects.
- Convert like measurement units within a given measurement system.
- Geometric measurement: understand concepts of area and relate area to multiplication and to addition.
- Geometric measurement: understand concepts of volume and relate volume to multi-

plication and to addition.
- Represent and interpret data.

Geometry
- Identify and describe shapes.
- Analyze, compare, create, and compose shapes.

6. Allow students to present their information in bulleted lists using technology to help with note taking.
7. Present the information in a multi-media format rather than using posters.

Resources:

Rocks and minerals explanation
http://education.usgs.gov/primary.html#rocks

Introduction to rocks and minerals
http://geomaps.wr.usgs.gov/parks/rxmin/rock.html

Activities and modules about rocks and minerals
http://education.usgs.gov/primary.html#rocks

Rock and mineral information
http://www.rocksforkids.com/RFK/identification.html

Exemplar Texts:

Explore Rocks and Minerals!: 25 Great Projects, Activities, Experiments.
By Cynthia Light Brown and Nick Brown. Nomad Press, 2010. 96p. (9781934670613)
Grade Level: 3–6
Lexile Level: 920L
Dewey: 551

Mighty Minerals.
By Christine Peterson. ABDO, 2010. 24p. (9781604537444)
Grade Level: 3–5
ATOS Reading Level: 4.6
Dewey: 549

Rocks & Minerals.
By Melvin Berger and Gilda Berger. Scholastic, 2010. 48p. (9780545202053)
Grade Level: 2–4
ATOS Reading Level: 4.2
Lexile Level: 780L
Dewey: 550

Rocks and Minerals.
By Kathleen Weidner Zoehfeld. National Geographic, 2012. 32p. (9781426310393)
Grade Level: K–3
ATOS Reading Level: 3.6
Lexile Level: 550L
Dewey: 552

Smashing Science Projects About Earth's Rocks and Minerals.
By Robert Gardner. Enslow, 2007. 48p. (9780766027312)
Grade Level: 3–5
ATOS Reading Level: 4.8
Dewey: 552.078

9

The Shocking Truth about Energy

By Loreen Leedy. Holiday House, 2010. 32p. (9780823422203)

Grade Level: 3–5 *(Grades K–2 with modifications)*
ATOS Reading Level: 5.1
Lexile Level: AD 720L (Adult Directed)
Dewey: 333.79
Subject Area: science, language arts

Essential Question: Where does energy come from?

Unit Summary: Students will examine the essential question, "Where does energy come from?" They will identify the energy sources they already know as the teacher lists them on a chart. After listening to the book, they will add the remaining sources to the list. Next the students will conduct independent research in small groups to complete a graphic organizer showing the pros and cons of a variety of renewable and nonrenewable sources. They will work in collaborative groups to investigate their energy source and later present their findings orally or through the use of technology.

Vocabulary: algae, atoms, carbon dioxide, electricity, energy, fuel, geothermal, global warming, motion, muscle, nonrenewable, plankton, pollution, prehistoric, renewable, sound, turbine

Approximate lesson time: two to three class periods

Common Core State Standards (55 total)

Reading Standards (8)

Key Ideas and Details

1. Read closely to determine what the text says explicitly and to make logical inferences from it; cite specific textual evidence when writing or speaking to support conclusions drawn from the text.

2. Determine central ideas or themes of a text and analyze their development; summarize the key supporting details and ideas.

Craft and Structure

4. Interpret words and phrases as they are used in a text, including determining technical, connotative, and figurative meanings, and analyze how specific

word choices shape meaning or tone.

6. Assess how point of view or purpose shapes the content and style of a text.

Integration of Knowledge and Ideas

7. Integrate and evaluate content presented in diverse media and formats, including visually and quantitatively, as well as in words.

8. Delineate and evaluate the argument and specific claims in a text, including the validity of the reasoning as well as the relevance and sufficiency of the evidence.

9. Analyze how two or more texts address similar themes or topics in order to build knowledge or to compare the approaches the authors take.

Range of Reading and Level of Text Complexity

10. Read and comprehend complex literary and informational texts independently and proficiently.

Writing Standards (9)

Text Types and Purposes

1. Write arguments to support claims in an analysis of substantive topics or texts, using valid reasoning and relevant and sufficient evidence.

Booktalk: Flip a wall switch and instantly you have light. Punch a button and the television springs to life. Press the computer button and turn on the monitor. Everything electric is right at hand with the flip of a switch. Electricity is a form of energy and it's something we use every day. We get it in many different ways. So where does our energy come from? Let's take a closer look at energy with the book *The Shocking Truth about Energy.*

Book Time

1. Discuss energy-saving ideas with the students. List them on a chart. Alternatively, have them discuss ideas about saving energy in small groups and then make the class list.
2. Share the booktalk for *The Shocking Truth about Energy* (above).
3. Tell the students to listen for the different sources that make electricity and also to see if they can learn new ways to save energy.
4. Read the book to the students.
5. Add the energy-saving suggestions they learned from the book to the class chart. Discuss the value of saving energy and how they can help.
6. Review the essential question and discuss the answers.

✎ *Suggested lesson break.*

Library Activity

I Need Some Energy!

I. Materials: notebook paper, books about sources of energy, computer access with suggested links to energy information, suggested technology presentation ideas other than the oral presentation (your own list depending on your media resources), graphic organizer

II. Instructions

1. Ask the students to name the sources of energy that they know and list them where everyone can see. Make sure these sources are covered by including them if the students don't know them: petroleum (oil),

natural gas, nuclear power, solar power, wind, water (hydroelectric), geothermal, and plant power (biofuels).

2. Tell them they will be researching one form of energy and listing all the ways it is helpful and all the ways it is harmful to the earth.

3. Decide if you want the student groups to choose their own energy form or if you will assign each group a source to research. The assignment may also be done individually.

4. Inform the groups that you want everyone to write down the group's findings.

III. Procedure

1. Give each student a graphic organizer.

2. Instruct them to write the name of their energy source as the title. Ask them to identify whether their source is renewable or nonrenewable in the title or under it.

3. Explain how to use the graphic organizer. Point out the Helpful column and the Harmful column and review an example from the book. For example, fossil fuels would have "makes a great deal of heat" under the helpful column but they would write "will run out" under the harmful column.

4. Allow time for the students to look up information about their energy topics using the books or selected links or databases. Refer back to the book for the lower grades.

✐ *Suggested lesson break.*

5. Instruct the students to get together in their energy groups (if they worked independently) and take turns reading their column entries to share their findings. Tell them to add in any new ideas they learn.

6. Choose one student from each energy source to read the list to the rest of the class or incorporate technology and have each group use it to make the presentations to the class.

7. Each student will write down two to three important facts about the other energy sources.

8. Review the essential question and discuss the answers.

2. Write informative/explanatory texts to examine and convey complex ideas and information clearly and accurately through the effective selection, organization, and analysis of content.

Production and Distribution of Writing

4. Produce clear and coherent writing in which the development, organization, and style are appropriate to task, purpose, and audience.

5. Develop and strengthen writing as needed by planning, revising, editing, rewriting, or trying a new approach.

6. Use technology, including the Internet, to produce and publish writing and to interact and collaborate with others.

Research to Build and Present Knowledge

7. Conduct short as well as more sustained research projects based on focused questions, demonstrating understanding of the subject under investigation.

8. Gather relevant information from multiple print and digital sources, assess the credibility and accuracy of each source, and integrate the information while avoiding plagiarism.

9. Draw evidence from literary or informational texts to support analysis, reflection, and research.

Range of Writing

10. Write routinely over extended time frames (time for research, reflection, and revision) and shorter time frames (a single sitting or a day or two) for a range of tasks, purposes, and audiences.

Speaking and Listening Standards (6)

Comprehension and Collaboration

1. Prepare for and participate effectively in a range of conversations and collaborations with diverse partners, building on others' ideas and expressing their own clearly and persuasively.

2. Integrate and evaluate information presented in diverse media and formats, including visually, quantitatively, and orally.

3. Evaluate a speaker's point of view, reasoning, and use of evidence and rhetoric.

Presentation of Knowledge and Ideas

4. Present information, findings, and supporting evidence such that listeners can follow the line of reasoning and the organization, development, and

IV. Reflect
1. Have the students read over the lists they made for the group's source.
2. Ask them to circle the most important idea they learned from each column.
3. Then ask them to number the ideas in order of importance. The circled fact will be number 1, and they will put a "2" by the second most important fact, and so on.

VI. Assessment
Choice 1
Have the students put away their energy lists of helpful and harmful facts. Let them write a two-paragraph review about their energy source. They will also state if their source is renewable or nonrenewable.
Choice 2
Without using their information, have each student make a list of helpful and harmful effects of their energy source.

Collaborative Teacher Activity

Green or Mean?

I. Materials: notebook paper, list from library research by each student
II. Instructions
1. Ask the students to name the sources of electricity they studied in the library and list them where everyone can see. Make sure these sources are covered: petroleum (oil), natural gas, nuclear power, solar power, wind, water (hydroelectric), geothermal, and plant power (biofuels).
2. Tell them they will be writing to explain their energy source, how it is helpful and harmful, and why they think it is a good or bad energy source to use.
III. Procedure
1. Have each student take out a piece of notebook paper and title it with the energy source they researched.
2. Each student will write two to three paragraphs about their energy source to define and explain its positive and negative as-

pects. They will give their opinion as to whether it is a good source to use or has too many problems and tell why. They will support the idea they present using their research from the library and their graphic organizer information. They will include the use of linking words like *because, therefore, since, for example* to connect their opinion to their facts. They will end with a concluding paragraph explaining why their energy source is a good one or harmful one to use.

IV. Reflect
1. Have each student silently read over his or her writing.
2. Choose volunteers to read their papers aloud to the class representing each energy source studied.
3. Give the students time to make additions to their papers.
4. In pairs, have each student read his or her partner's paper.
5. Discuss the arguments to make sure each one supports the opinion of the writer in their energy groups or as a class.

VI. Assessment
Choice 1
Use the papers written in class as a first draft. Ask the students to rewrite their papers and turn them in.
Choice 2
Without using their information, have students explain the helpful and harmful effects of their energy source.

Extension Activities

1. Create a class chart that shows in a simple way the positive and negative impact of each energy source in the book.
2. Have each student make a chart, diagram, or cause-and-result example to illustrate their energy source.
3. Research energy to find out how much energy is produced in the U.S. from each source and create a bar graph or pie chart to illustrate it.

style are appropriate to task, purpose, and audience.

5. Make strategic use of digital media and visual displays of data to express information and enhance understanding of presentations.

6. Adapt speech to a variety of contexts and communicative tasks, demonstrating command of formal English when indicated or appropriate.

Language Standards (6)

Conventions of Standard English

1. Demonstrate command of the conventions of standard English grammar and usage when writing or speaking.

2. Demonstrate command of the conventions of standard English capitalization, punctuation, and spelling when writing.

Knowledge of Language

3. Apply knowledge of language to understand how language functions in different contexts, to make effective choices for meaning or style, and to comprehend more fully when reading or listening.

Vocabulary Acquisition and Use

4. Determine or clarify the meaning of unknown and

multiple-meaning words and phrases by using context clues, analyzing meaningful word parts, and consulting general and specialized reference materials, as appropriate.

5. Demonstrate understanding of figurative language, word relationships, and nuances in word meanings.

6. Acquire and use accurately a range of general academic and domain-specific words and phrases sufficient for reading, writing, speaking, and listening at the college and career readiness level; demonstrate independence in gathering vocabulary knowledge when encountering an unknown term important to comprehension or expression.

Mathematical Practices (7)

1. Make sense of problems and persevere in solving them.

2. Reason abstractly and quantitatively.

3. Construct viable arguments and critique the reasoning of others.

4. Model with mathematics.

5. Use appropriate tools strategically.

6. Attend to precision.

4. Set up a class or school project to reduce the amount of energy used or that shows ways to conserve energy at school.

5. After reading the book, have the students write a short description of the main idea of the book. Use the phrase, "I am a scientist. I know that _____."

Modifications for Grades K–2

1. Write the names of the energy sources on a pre-prepared graphic organizer.

2. As you read the book, have the students draw each kind of energy to help them remember it or write down a few words to remember the energy source and to also show the pros and cons.

3. After reading the book, discuss ways to save energy and have them act out or draw pictures of ways they can save energy.

4. Write a short phrase for each energy-saving method for the students to add to their paper so they better understand the ideas.

5. Create a class list for suggestions about saving energy.

Differentiation strategies:

1. Discuss, define, or review the vocabulary after reading the book. Point out examples of how the words were used.

2. Identify or list the links that are available to help them locate their energy information.

3. Use the graphic organizer that includes the energy sources and read the book a second time. Stop and guide the students as they take notes for each energy source.

4. Have one record keeper in each group to write the information.

5. Use strategic grouping by working in small groups.

6. Allow students to present their graphic organizers in other ways, including through the use of technology.

7. Increase or reduce the number of helpful and harmful facts each student or group needs to collect.

Resources:

About energy sources
http://www.eia.gov/kids/energy.cfm?page=2

About energy
http://www.energyquest.ca.gov/story/

Renewable energy sources
http://www.alliantenergykids.com/EnergyandThe
    Environment/RenewableEnergy/index.htm

Interactive game about energy sources
http://www.eschooltoday.com/what-is-energy-for
    -children.html

Exemplar Texts:

Aliens and Energy.
By Agnieszka Jòzefina Biskup. Capstone Press, 2012.
    32p. (9781429673259)
Grade Level: 3–5
ATOS Reading Level: 5.1
Lexile Level: GN790L
Dewey: 530

Energy Is Everywhere.
By June Young. Children's Press, 2006. 32p.
    (9780516280035)
Grade Level: PreK–1
Lexile Level: 50L
Dewey: 531.6

Forms of Energy.
By Anna Claybourne. Heinemann, 2010. 48p.
    (9781410933775)
Grade Level: 4–8.
ATOS Reading Level: 6.4
Lexile Level: 790L
Dewey: 531.6

The Kids' Solar Energy Book.
By Tilly Spetgang and Malcolm Wells. Imagine Pub.,
    2009. 24p. (9780982306413)
Grade Level: 3–5
Lexile Level: 790L
Dewey: 333.7923

7. Look for and make use of structure.

Mathematical Content (19)

Counting and Cardinality

- Count to tell the number of objects.
- Compare numbers.

Operations and Algebraic Thinking

- Represent and solve problems involving addition and subtraction.
- Generate and analyze patterns.
- Write and interpret numerical expressions.
- Analyze patterns and relationships.

Number and Operations in Base Ten

- Solve problems involving the four operations, and identify and explain patterns in arithmetic.
- Use place value understanding and properties of operations to perform multi-digit arithmetic.
- Gain familiarity with factors and multiples.
- Perform operations with multi-digit whole numbers and with decimals to hundredths.

Number and Operations—Fractions

- Develop understanding of fractions as numbers.

- Extend understanding of fraction equivalence and ordering.
- Build fractions from unit fractions by applying and extending previous understandings of operations on whole numbers.
- Understand decimal notation for fractions, and compare decimal fractions.
- Use equivalent fractions as a strategy to add and subtract fractions.

Measurement and Data

- Describe and compare measurable attributes.
- Classify objects and count the number of objects in categories.
- Represent and interpret data.

Geometry

- Graph points on the coordinate plane to solve real-world and mathematical problems.

Timeless Thomas: How Thomas Edison Changed Our Lives. By Gene Barretta. Henry Holt, 2012. 40p. (9780805091083)
Grade Level: 4–7
ATOS Reading Level: 5.5
Lexile Level: 900L
Dewey: 621.3092

PART III

Teaching Technology in Your Library

Technology is . . .

Definition: taking and using scientific knowledge in a practical way; used particularly in industry.

Background

Technology involves practical applications of science, as well as being a term used to describe the machines and equipment that aid in the application of engineering and science to solve problems. Computers often spring to mind when technology is mentioned, but the range is far more encompassing than information technology.

Technology encompasses a wide field of breakthroughs: using nanotechnology at the subatomic level, producing more efficient solar panels, developing speedier digital processing, manufacturing medical tools, using stem cells to increase the chances of older women having a baby, cloning to grow new organs, simplifying genetic testing, creating changes in Facebook, and much more.

Technology is constantly tested, scrutinized, reworked, and improved until it fits the needs of a changing world. It has the possibility to transform any discipline, and each application of technology holds the possibility to change the world.

10

Forces and Motion at Work

By Shirley Duke. Rourke Publishing, 2012. 48p. (9781617417887)

Grade Level: 3–5 *(Grades K–2 with modifications)*
ATOS Reading Level: 5.2
Guided Reading Level: W
Dewey: 531.6
Subject Area: technology, science, writing

Essential Question: What makes forces and motions on Earth?

Unit Summary: Students will examine the essential question, "What makes forces and motions on Earth?" by researching information from a variety of sources relating to the vocabulary of forces and motion. They will summarize their information and then reduce their facts into a short statement of less than one hundred and forty characters in a style suitable for Twitter. From an assigned list of words, each group of students will use print and online information to define their word, read about it to identify and comprehend the scientific principle, and collect facts relating to that principle. The groups will narrow the information by wording it in a phrase or sentence that fits Twitter's parameters. They will share their information in the library in a way that is accessible for the available technology there or in a class PowerPoint presentation designed to look like a tweet on Twitter.

Vocabulary: accelerate, aerodynamics, centrifugal force, centripetal force, deform, drag, electromagnets,

Common Core State Standards (45 total)

Reading Standards (7)

Key Ideas and Details

1. Read closely to determine what the text says explicitly and to make logical inferences from it; cite specific textual evidence when writing or speaking to support conclusions drawn from the text.

2. Determine central ideas or themes of a text and analyze their development; summarize the key supporting details and ideas.

Craft and Structure

4. Interpret words and phrases as they are used in a text, including determining technical, connotative, and figurative meanings, and analyze how specific

word choices shape meaning or tone.

5. Analyze the structure of texts, including how specific sentences, paragraphs, and larger portions of the text (e.g., a section, chapter, scene, or stanza) relate to each other and the whole.

6. Assess how point of view or purpose shapes the content and style of a text.

Integration of Knowledge and Ideas

7. Integrate and evaluate content presented in diverse media and formats, including visually and quantitatively, as well as in words.

Range of Reading and Level of Text Complexity

10. Read and comprehend complex literary and informational texts independently and proficiently.

Writing Standards (9)

Text Types and Purposes

2. Write informative/explanatory texts to examine and convey complex ideas and information clearly and accurately through the effective selection, organization, and analysis of content.

3. Write narratives to develop real or imagined experiences or events using effective technique,

forces, friction, gravity, inertia, kinetic energy, magnets, mechanics, potential energy, recoil resistance

Approximate lesson time: two to three class periods

Booktalk: Who has ridden a roller coaster? Think about what it felt like when you made the turns, and when you came flying down a steep hill. Forces act on us all the time. Often they aren't as exciting as riding a roller coaster, but they act on us just the same. What keeps us on Earth? Why do balls stop rolling? How do technology and forces make our life easier to manage? There are sets of laws in science that explain forces and motion. Take a look at the book, *Forces and Motion at Work.*

Book Time

1. Share the booktalk for *Forces and Motion at Work* (above).
2. Post the vocabulary and ask the students to listen for those words, and try to relate them to something in the world that they know.
3. Read the book aloud.

 Library Activity

Tweet Facts

I.   Materials: books about forces and motion, computers, writing materials, technology to display work, graphic organizer
II. Instructions
   1. Tell the students they will be investigating the vocabulary word they are assigned.
   2. Read the word list and ask them to explain any of the words they know.
   3. Tell the students they will research their word and present the information they learn in a way that is compatible with Twitter. Explain the idea behind Twitter and talk about communicating in short sentences.
   4. Define character and show them an example of a message. Demonstrate how to count the characters. Explain that Twitter limits the message to less than one hundred and forty characters.

III. Procedure
1. Practice writing a message that is less than one hundred and forty characters by having the students compose one about what they like to do in their free time.
2. Read some of the messages aloud and discuss the limits they encountered.
3. Assign the listed vocabulary to individuals or students who will work in small groups.
4. The students will look up information about that word using a variety of sources.
5. Make notes about the information related to that word.
6. Identify the main idea about how their word is related to forces and motion.
7. Write that idea in a Twitter message. Ask each student to word it individually and then collaborate to form a single message from each group.

✎ *Suggested lesson break.*

8. Discuss the ways Twitter might affect how information is spread today. Write down those ideas.
9. Post their message using the technology you have chosen. Read through the information.
10. Discuss the essential question and related the answers to the vocabulary in the lesson.

IV. Reflect
1. Have the students review the individual messages they first wrote and compare it to the single group message.
2. Ask them to think about the difficulty of finding the main idea and getting the meaning across in a short message.

V. Assessment
Choice 1
Write a paragraph about the process of summarizing their facts into one short message and explain the pros and cons of spreading information in such a short, tight manner.
Choice 2
Print a page of the messages and give a copy to each student. Ask the students to choose two or three messages from definitions they didn't write and better explain the word in a

well-chosen details, and well-structured event sequences.

Production and Distribution of Writing

4. Produce clear and coherent writing in which the development, organization, and style are appropriate to task, purpose, and audience.

5. Develop and strengthen writing as needed by planning, revising, editing, rewriting, or trying a new approach.

6. Use technology, including the Internet, to produce and publish writing and to interact and collaborate with others.

Research to Build and Present Knowledge

7. Conduct short as well as more sustained research projects based on focused questions, demonstrating understanding of the subject under investigation.

8. Gather relevant information from multiple print and digital sources, assess the credibility and accuracy of each source, and integrate the information while avoiding plagiarism.

9. Draw evidence from literary or informational texts to support analysis, reflection, and research.

Range of Writing

10. Write routinely over extended time frames (time for research, reflection, and revision) and shorter time frames (a single sitting or a day or two) for a range of tasks, purposes, and audiences.

Speaking and Listening Standards (6)

Comprehension and Collaboration

1. Prepare for and participate effectively in a range of conversations and collaborations with diverse partners, building on others' ideas and expressing their own clearly and persuasively.

2. Integrate and evaluate information presented in diverse media and formats, including visually, quantitatively, and orally.

3. Evaluate a speaker's point of view, reasoning, and use of evidence and rhetoric.

Presentation of Knowledge and Ideas

4. Present information, findings, and supporting evidence such that listeners can follow the line of reasoning and the organization, development, and style are appropriate to task, purpose, and audience.

short paragraph. The final paragraph will be an explanation of the shortcomings of using a brief message.

Collaborative Teacher Activity

Blog All About It

I. Materials: computer; three to five blog templates from a chosen blog provider, such as WordPress, Blogger, or LiveJournal; writing materials; reference materials or library notes

II. Instructions
   1. The students will be writing a class blog. They will vote on the design for the blog from the choices you pre-selected.
   2. Each group will post about their assigned word to provide information and art that illustrates their concept. They will also include a short biography on a page you've set up for author information. You might include a digital photo of the authors and have the students add it to their presentation slide.
   3. Tell the students how you plan to have them post. You can set up the blog and pre-set the dates or each group can post on its assigned day.
   4. Review each blog to introduce the concepts and give the students time to comment or ask questions either orally or on the blog itself.

III. Activity
   1. Review Internet safety and the rules you have for computer use in your classroom.
   2. Show the blog template choices and conduct a vote. You might model how to use the site by posting the assignment and schedule on it.
   3. Have the students assemble into their groups and prepare their blog post using new information or their library notes.
   4. Ask each student to write a short author biography to include on the author page.

✎ *Suggested lesson break.*

5. Post the vocabulary information as they are ready.

6. Allow time to find art to include in their posts.

7. Present the blog information and let the students add their comments on the blog.

IV. Reflection

1. Have each student review his or her own group's post following the last group's post.

2. Ask the students to write down what they might do differently if they posted again.

V. Assessment

Choice 1

Assess the blog post of each group according to the criteria you have determined before the lesson.

Choice 2

Have the students choose two or three vocabulary words and explain them.

Extension Activities

1. Make a class Wiki and put their information on it.
(URL for setting up wiki: http://www.central desktop.com/l?sr=cj&sy=wiki)

2. Do an activity using the concepts behind simple machines and illustrate them.

3. Do a podcast about the vocabulary by writing the script in their groups and recording the information. Compare this method of communicating to other means of communicating.

4. After reading the book, have the students write a short description of the main idea of the book. Use the phrase, "I am a technology specialist. I know that _____."

Modifications for Grades 1–2

1. Assign select vocabulary words to the groups and look them up in a dictionary.

2. Then have the students find their word and read about it in two other resources.

3. Have them find a picture that represents their word. Present their information by putting it in a simple Twitter-style message.

5. Make strategic use of digital media and visual displays of data to express information and enhance understanding of presentations.

6. Adapt speech to a variety of contexts and communicative tasks, demonstrating command of formal English when indicated or appropriate.

Language Standards (6)

Conventions of Standard English

1. Demonstrate command of the conventions of standard English grammar and usage when writing or speaking.

2. Demonstrate command of the conventions of standard English capitalization, punctuation, and spelling when writing.

Knowledge of Language

3. Apply knowledge of language to understand how language functions in different contexts, to make effective choices for meaning or style, and to comprehend more fully when reading or listening.

Vocabulary Acquisition and Use

4. Determine or clarify the meaning of unknown and multiple-meaning words and phrases by using context clues, analyzing meaningful word parts,

and consulting general and specialized reference materials, as appropriate.

5. Demonstrate understanding of figurative language, word relationships, and nuances in word meanings.

6. Acquire and use accurately a range of general academic and domain-specific words and phrases sufficient for reading, writing, speaking, and listening at the college and career readiness level; demonstrate independence in gathering vocabulary knowledge when encountering an unknown term important to comprehension or expression.

Mathematical Practices (6)

1. Make sense of problems and persevere in solving them.

2. Reason abstractly and quantitatively.

3. Construct viable arguments and critique the reasoning of others.

5. Use appropriate tools strategically.

6. Attend to precision.

7. Look for and make use of structure.

4. Put the tweets up where everyone can see them.
5. Read them.
6. Then return to the book and review how the vocabulary word was used there.

Differentiation strategies:

1. Discuss, define, or review the vocabulary before reading the book. Point out examples of how the words were used. Use fewer vocabulary words by eliminating the more difficult words.
2. Identify or list the links that are available to help them locate their information.
3. Pull relevant books and have them displayed.
4. Discuss the possible means of using technology available in your media center.
5. Use strategic grouping by working in small groups.
6. Present their information orally rather than creating the blog or twitter message.
7. Give each group more than one vocabulary word.

Resources:

Information and definitions about forces and motion
http://library.thinkquest.org/CR0215468/force_and
_motion.htm

Information and examples about forces
http://www.physics4kids.com/files/motion_force.html

Activities, games, and interactive lessons about forces and motion
http://classroom.jc-schools.net/sci-units/force.htm#1
(lower grades)

Interactive activities about forces and motions
http://www.learningscience.org/psc2bmotionforces
.htm

Specific information on different forces
http://sciencespot.net/Pages/kdzphysics.html

Setting up a Wiki
http://www.centraldesktop.com/l?sr=cj&sy=wiki

Exemplar Texts:

Balance and Motion: Toying with Gravity.
By Emily Sohn and Joseph Brennan. Norwood, 2011.
   24p. (9781599534053)
Grade Level: 2–5
ATOS Reading Level: 3.1
Lexile Level: 450L
Dewey: 531

Experiments with Motion.
By Susan H. Gray. Scholastic, 2012. 48p.
   (9780531263464)
Grade Level: 4–6
ATOS Reading Level: 5.1
Lexile Level: 690L
Dewey: 531

Motion.
By Ellen Lawrence. Bearport, 2013. 24p. (9781617727399)
Grade Level: PreK–3
Lexile Level: IG 720L
Dewey: 531

Science Lab: Motion and Forces.
By Rebecca Hirsch. Cherry Lake, 2012. 32p.
   (9781610802055)
Grade Level: 4–8
ATOS Reading Level: 5.2
Dewey: 531

Zombies and Forces and Motion.
By Mark Andrew Weakland. Capstone, 2011. 32p.
   (9781429665773)
Grade Level: 4–7
ATOS Reading Level: 4.4
Lexile Level: GN 740L
Dewey: 531

Mathematical Content (11)

Counting and Cardinality
- Count to tell the number of objects.
- Compare numbers.

Operations and Algebraic Thinking
- Represent and solve problems involving addition and subtraction.
- Analyze patterns and relationships.

Number and Operations in Base Ten
- Understand place value.
- Use place value understanding and properties of operations to add and subtract.

Measurement and Data
- Describe and compare measurable attributes.
- Classify objects and count the number of objects in categories.
- Measure lengths indirectly and by iterating length units.
- Tell and write time.
- Represent and interpret data.

11

High-Tech Olympics

By Nick Hunter. Heinemann Library, 2011. 48p. (9781410941213)

Grade Level: 3–5 *(Grades K–2 with modifications)*
ATOS Reading Level: 6.4
Lexile Level: 970L
Dewey: 796.48
Subject Area: mathematics, science, reading

Essential Question: What are Olympic distances really like?

Unit Summary: Students will examine the essential question, "What are Olympic distances really like?" Students will be grouped into five teams and given an identifying number or name. They will use an Olympic record database to locate distances, lengths, or heights of sports in the track and field events and record them. Then they will measure the equivalent distance in the library, classroom, or hallways and mark the distance with a sticky note to show the measurement. They will compare their results and discuss them.

Vocabulary: air resistance, amputees, ancient, bindings, carbohydrates, fiberglass, gears, monitors, Olympics, Paralympics, proteins, spikes, streamlined, synchronized, technology

Approximate lesson time: one to two class periods

Booktalk: Have you ever dreamed of winning an Olympic medal? Athletes around the world have worked hard to win a gold, silver, or bronze medal and become the best athlete in their sport. However, today much more than practice has to happen to become an elite athlete.

Common Core State Standards (53 total)

Reading Standards (7)

Key Ideas and Details

1. Read closely to determine what the text says explicitly and to make logical inferences from it; cite specific textual evidence when writing or speaking to support conclusions drawn from the text.

2. Determine central ideas or themes of a text and analyze their development; summarize the key supporting details and ideas.

3. Analyze how and why individuals, events, and ideas develop and interact over the course of a text.

Craft and Structure

4. Interpret words and phrases as they are used in a text, including determining technical, connotative,

and figurative meanings, and analyze how specific word choices shape meaning or tone.

Integration of Knowledge and Ideas

7. Integrate and evaluate content presented in diverse media and formats, including visually and quantitatively, as well as in words.

8. Delineate and evaluate the argument and specific claims in a text, including the validity of the reasoning as well as the relevance and sufficiency of the evidence.

Range of Reading and Level of Text Complexity

10. Read and comprehend complex literary and informational texts independently and proficiently.

Writing Standards (10)

Text Types and Purposes

1. Write arguments to support claims in an analysis of substantive topics or texts, using valid reasoning and relevant and sufficient evidence.

2. Write informative/ explanatory texts to examine and convey complex ideas and information clearly and accurately through the effective selection, organization, and analysis of content.

3. Write narratives to develop real or imagined

Let's find out what else it takes to become an Olympic athlete. We'll take a look at the book *High-Tech Olympics* to see what goes into becoming a world class athlete.

Book Time

1. Share the booktalk for *High-Tech Olympics* (above).
2. Read the main text of the book without including the sidebars.
3. Return to the book and point out the Olympic events, particularly those in the sidebars, that cover a specific distance or height.
4. Review the metric system. Ask the students to notice the units used for the races (meters). Show them a meter stick.

Library Activity

Olympic Distances in Our School

I. Materials: different colored sticky notes or nonstick tape (like the blue tape painters use); meter sticks; writing materials; list of distances from various years (students choose from Olympic site database); graphic organizer listing the six sports: high jump, pole vault, long jump, triple jump, shot put, and javelin throw

II. Instructions

1. Tell the students they will be investigating distances and heights in Olympic sports. The groups will mark those distances or heights in the library or hallway. Point out the list of six sports on the graphic organizer. After they complete the measuring, they will locate statistics about winners in any seven past games for one of the sports they just measured.

2. Divide the students into groups of three or four. Assign each group an identifying number or name (or have the students choose their own group name).

3. Using the Olympic site database (http://www.databaseolympics.com/), the students will look up the distances for each of the six following summer game sports for both men and women in 2008: high jump, pole vault, long jump, triple jump, shot put,

and javelin throw. After opening the website, select 2008 and click on it. On that page, scroll down to the sports section. Click on track and field.

4. The students will record the twelve distances on their organizers and then use meter sticks to measure those distances in the library and hallway. They will mark each distance with a sticky note. Groups will put the event and group number on each sticky note they use.

5. Last, they will look up and record the statistics of the first-place winners in one of the listed sports in five different Olympic games and record their times, distances, or heights. This time they may choose from any year listed. This part can be done in their groups or individually. These statistics will be used in the collaborative teacher activity. (You might choose to skip this activity if the collaborative activity isn't being done.)

III.   Procedure

1. Have each group look up and record the statistics for both men and women in each sport listed for 2008. Then measure the twelve distances or heights of their sport in the library or hallway.

2. Each group will mark their measurements with the sticky note holding their group number and event.

3. When each group finishes measuring, they should prepare for the next activity. Pass out the second graphic organizer. Have them begin the next activity until all groups are finished measuring. See Step 6 for details.

4. Call the groups back together. Ask each team to share their results. Compare the distances to make sure each team was measuring accurately.

✐ *Suggested lesson break.*

5. For the next step, students will collect data to use with the collaborating teacher as all the groups finish measuring. Have the students look up past Olympic Games from the same website and choose one sport from those they

experiences or events using effective technique, well-chosen details, and well-structured event sequences.

Production and Distribution of Writing

4. Produce clear and coherent writing in which the development, organization, and style are appropriate to task, purpose, and audience.

5. Develop and strengthen writing as needed by planning, revising, editing, rewriting, or trying a new approach.

6. Use technology, including the Internet, to produce and publish writing and to interact and collaborate with others.

Research to Build and Present Knowledge

7. Conduct short as well as more sustained research projects based on focused questions, demonstrating understanding of the subject under investigation.

8. Gather relevant information from multiple print and digital sources, assess the credibility and accuracy of each source, and integrate the information while avoiding plagiarism.

9. Draw evidence from literary or informational texts to support analysis, reflection, and research.

Range of Writing

10. Write routinely over extended time frames (time for research, reflection, and revision) and shorter time frames (a single sitting or a day or two) for a range of tasks, purposes, and audiences.

Speaking and Listening Standards (5)

Comprehension and Collaboration

1. Prepare for and participate effectively in a range of conversations and collaborations with diverse partners, building on others' ideas and expressing their own clearly and persuasively.

2. Integrate and evaluate information presented in diverse media and formats, including visually, quantitatively, and orally.

Presentation of Knowledge and Ideas

4. Present information, findings, and supporting evidence such that listeners can follow the line of reasoning and the organization, development, and style are appropriate to task, purpose, and audience.

5. Make strategic use of digital media and visual displays of data to express information and enhance understanding of presentations.

just measured. They will record the statistics of the first place winners from each of five years in one of the sports that they just measured. They will record their times, distances, or heights. Tell the students to include the person's name, country, and year they won as well as their winning distance. This might be done as a group with one record keeper or have each student keep a data sheet.

6. Collect the graphic organizers and pass them along to the collaborating teacher.

7. Lead a discussion about the essential question.

IV. Reflect

1. Have the students write down something that impressed or surprised them as they measured.

2. Ask all groups to look at one of the distances they measured and picture that distance outside.

3. Have the groups remove their sticky notes.

V. Assessment

Choice 1

Monitor the groups as they work and check one of their measurements.

Choice 2

Have the students choose three of their measurements and write a description of how long it was in relation to something concrete to compare the height and help them visualize it. For example, a 2.06 meter length would be about the height of a tall adult man.

Collaborative Teacher Activity

Olympic Winners and the Metric System

I. Materials: graph paper, writing paper, Olympic winner game statistics from library work, metric system information: http://www.vision learning.com/library/module_viewer.php? mid=47

Database for classroom teacher http://www .databaseolympics.com/

II. Instructions
1. Tell the students they will create a line graph to show the gold medal winners from seven different Olympic Games in their chosen sport.
2. Next, they will take a metric unit related to their sport and convert it within the metric system to the next unit, both up and down. For example, if measuring meters, they will also convert it to centimeters and kilometers.
3. Last, they will create five word problems using the decimal measurements.

III. Activity
1. Review graphing that shows a change over time. Remind them to use a line graph to show the changes in time of their sport.
2. Allow enough time to complete the graphs. Make sure they include the year on the X axis and the height or distance on the Y axis.
3. Review the metric system. Have the students make a chart to list the units for volume, distance, and weight. Ask them to make their charts or lists in ascending order. You may want to review metric terms here: http://lamar.colostate.edu/~hillger/common.html.
4. Review how to move up by 10 or down by 10 by moving the decimal point to the appropriate unit. For example, if the distance in the high jump is 2.36 meters, they will take 2.36 meters and convert it to 236 centimeters (100 cm = 1 m) and .00236 kilometers (divide by 100).
5. Use the back of their graphs to show their metric conversions.

✎ *Suggested lesson break.*

6. Use their statistics from the graphs to create five word problems using the decimals to the nearest 100th. Remind them to show their answers.
7. Write a conclusion about differences in the statistics of that sport through the years and make an inference about why there have been changes in it over the years.

6. Adapt speech to a variety of contexts and communicative tasks, demonstrating command of formal English when indicated or appropriate.

Language Standards (5)

Conventions of Standard English

1. Demonstrate command of the conventions of standard English grammar and usage when writing or speaking.

2. Demonstrate command of the conventions of standard English capitalization, punctuation, and spelling when writing.

Knowledge of Language

3. Apply knowledge of language to understand how language functions in different contexts, to make effective choices for meaning or style, and to comprehend more fully when reading or listening.

Vocabulary Acquisition and Use

4. Determine or clarify the meaning of unknown and multiple-meaning words and phrases by using context clues, analyzing meaningful word parts, and consulting general and specialized reference materials, as appropriate.

6. Acquire and use accurately a range of general academic and domain-

specific words and phrases sufficient for reading, writing, speaking, and listening at the college and career readiness level; demonstrate independence in gathering vocabulary knowledge when encountering an unknown term important to comprehension or expression.

Mathematical Practices (8)

1. Make sense of problems and persevere in solving them.

2. Reason abstractly and quantitatively.

3. Construct viable arguments and critique the reasoning of others.

4. Model with mathematics.

5. Use appropriate tools strategically.

6. Attend to precision.

7. Look for and make use of structure.

8. Look for and express regularity in repeated reasoning.

Mathematical Content (18)

Counting and Cardinality

• Know number names and the count sequence.
• Compare numbers.

IV. Reflection
   1. Have the students review their graphs. Ask them to notice any trends they may see.
   2. Have volunteers share what they noticed.
V. Assessment
   Choice 1
      Present some selected word problems written by the students and have the class work them.
   Choice 2
      Assess the graphs and review the word problems.

Extension Activities

1. Have the students use their metric conversions and change them to standard units. Add another set of columns to the graphic organizer if you choose. Or have them use a metric calculator online (http://www.conversion-metric.org/).
2. Have the students use library resources to find out information about one of the chosen sports and learn how technology has improved the sport. Then have them write about the changes and use details to support their information.
3. Repeat the activity using information from the Paralympics games (http://www.paralympic.org/Results/paralympic-records/Athletics).
4. After reading the book, have the students write a short description of the main idea of the book. Use the phrase, "I am a technology specialist. I know that _____."

Modifications for Grades K–2

1. Review the metric system and show the students a centimeter and a meter using rulers and meter sticks.
2. Give the students the graphic organizer with the information already posted on it.
3. Reduce the number of events to three.
4. Have the students measure the distances in either all meters or centimeters after you round the distances to whole numbers on the graphic organizer.

5. Work together as a class to measure the distances.

Differentiation strategies:

1. Mark the places you want the students to post their five individual sports distances or lengths. For example, the high jump might be in one corner of the library. Post the name of the event there.
2. Choose another grouping of sports and have the students design a graphic organizer and record more data for that sport.
3. Have the students choose a fewer number of sports to fit the lesson into a shorter time frame.
4. For the collaborative activity, add or decrease the number of sports they will use for their research and graph.
5. Rather than collect the data to use in the collaborative activity during the library class, the teacher can bring the students in to collect it as part of their lesson.
6. Pre-write the distances or heights on the graphic organizer for the students to measure in the library and halls.
7. Use strategic grouping by working in small groups.
8. Assign the individual sports and years for the collaborative activity.
9. Allow students to present their graphic organizers in other ways, including through the use of technology.
10. Discuss, define, or review the vocabulary after reading the book. Point out examples of how the words were used.

Resources:

Using the metric system and resources (funded by NSF)
http://www.visionlearning.com/library/module_
   viewer.php?mid=47

Review of the metric system
http://lamar.colostate.edu/~hillger/common.html

Olympics database
http://www.databaseolympics.com/

Operations and Algebraic Thinking
- Use the four operations with whole numbers to solve problems.
- Gain familiarity with factors and multiples.
- Generate and analyze patterns.
- Write and interpret numerical expressions.
- Analyze patterns and relationships.

Number and Operations in Base Ten
- Understand the place value system.
- Perform operations with multi-digit whole numbers and with decimals to hundredths.

Number and Operations—Fractions
- Develop understanding of fractions as numbers.
- Extend understanding of fraction equivalence and ordering.
- Build fractions from unit fractions by applying and extending previous understandings of operations on whole numbers.
- Understand decimal notation for fractions, and compare decimal fractions.

Measurement and Data
- Describe and compare measurable attributes.
- Measure and estimate lengths in standard units.
- Convert like measurement units within a

given measurement system.
- Represent and interpret data.

Geometry
- Graph points on the coordinate plane to solve real-world and mathematical problems.

Online metric conversion tool
http://www.conversion-metric.org/

Paralympics database
http://www.paralympic.org/Results/paralympic
 -records/Athletics

Exemplar Texts:

G Is for Gold Medal: An Olympics Alphabet.
By Brad Herzog. Sleeping Bear, 2011. 32p.
 (9781585364626)
Grade Level: 2–5
ATOS Reading Level: 7.3
Dewey: 796.48

Physical Feats & Failures.
By Dona Herweck Rice. Teacher Created Materials, 2012. 48p. (9781433348709)
Grade Level: 3–5
Lexile Level: 800L
Dewey: 796

There Goes Ted Williams: The Greatest Hitter Who Ever Lived.
By Matt Tavares. Candlewick, 2012. 40p. (9780763627898)
Grade Level: 2–5
ATOS Reading Level: 3.8
Lexile Level: AD 810L
Dewey: 796.357092

Touch the Sky: Alice Coachman, Olympic High Jumper.
By Ann Malaspina. Albert Whitman, 2012. 32p. (9780807580356)
Grade Level: 2–4
ATOS Reading Level: 3.6
Dewey: 796.42092

Yes, She Can! Women's Sports Pioneers.
By Glenn Stout. Houghton/Sandpiper, 2011. 128p. (9780547417257)
Grade Level: 4–7
ATOS Reading Level: 6.7
Lexile Level: 1040L
Dewey: 796.0922

12

Man on the Moon

By Anastasia Suen. Viking, 2002. 32p. (9780140565980)

Grade Level: 2–5 *(Grades K–1 with modifications)*
ATOS Reading Level: 2.2
Lexile Level: NC 860L (Non-Conforming)
Dewey: 629.45
Subject Area: science, technology

Essential Question: How have astronauts and space travel changed since the early space program?

Unit Summary: Students will examine the essential question, "How have astronauts and space travel changed since the early space program?" As they listen to you read the book, students will notice what equipment and items astronauts use and think about how images in a book contribute to a better understanding of the text. They will view images from the current space program and compare the changes they see in them to the space program in its early days. Using a picture from the text, students will describe the sensations that might result from a splash down and then discuss the changes they have learned taking place in the space program by writing about them or comparing them in a discussion.

Vocabulary: alarms, astronauts, capsule, controls, countdown, gadgets, land, lift off, linked up, loomed, rockets, space, spacecraft, splashed down, suited up, tower, visitors

Approximate lesson time: two to three class periods

Common Core State Standards (48 total)

Reading Standards (8)

Key Ideas and Details

1. Read closely to determine what the text says explicitly and to make logical inferences from it; cite specific textual evidence when writing or speaking to support conclusions drawn from the text.

2. Determine central ideas or themes of a text and analyze their development; summarize the key supporting details and ideas.

3. Analyze how and why individuals, events, and ideas develop and interact over the course of a text.

Craft and Structure

4. Interpret words and phrases as they are used in a text, including determining technical, connotative,

and figurative meanings, and analyze how specific word choices shape meaning or tone.

5. Analyze the structure of texts, including how specific sentences, paragraphs, and larger portions of the text (e.g., a section, chapter, scene, or stanza) relate to each other and the whole.

Integration of Knowledge and Ideas

7. Integrate and evaluate content presented in diverse media and formats, including visually and quantitatively, as well as in words.

8. Delineate and evaluate the argument and specific claims in a text, including the validity of the reasoning as well as the relevance and sufficiency of the evidence.

Range of Reading and Level of Text Complexity

10. Read and comprehend complex literary and informational texts independently and proficiently.

Writing Standards (10)

Text Types and Purposes

1. Write arguments to support claims in an analysis of substantive topics or texts, using valid reasoning and relevant and sufficient evidence.

Booktalk: Astronauts today are exploring space in many ways. Today both women and men live and work twenty-four hours a day at the International Space Station. They conduct science experiments, study life in space, and learn about how things work in space. But living and traveling in space wasn't always easy—and it still isn't. Astronauts need special equipment to live, work, and travel in space. Putting the first man on the moon was a scary experience, and not just for the astronauts. It takes many people and important technology to do anything in outer space. Did you know women didn't always have the choice to become an astronaut? Things have changed in space travel since the early days. Let's find out what early astronauts needed to travel and survive in space and then look at how things have changed. We'll begin by reading the book *Man on the Moon*.

Book Time

1. Share the booktalk for *Man on the Moon* (above).
2. Introduce the book *Man on the Moon* to the students. Point out the author and illustrator. Ask the students what this book might be about. Tell them to look for things needed for space travel and the places they went as you read the story to them the first time.
3. Read the book to the class.

 Library Activity

What's That?

I. Materials: *Man on the Moon*, NASA website images to project on screen, art supplies, graphic organizer

These websites will help you locate specific information as you go through the lesson.

a. Tour by Suni Williams of ISS.
http://www.nasa.gov/mission_pages/station/main/suni_iss_tour.html

b. Additional images from image gallery show more differences, especially #3, #9, and #40.
http://www.nasa.gov/multimedia/imagegallery/iotd.html

c. Women astronauts and changes
   http://womenshistory.about.com/od/avia-tionspace/ig/Women-Astronauts/
d. Astronaut clothing
   http://www.nasa.gov/audience/for students/k-4/playandlearn/best-dressed -astronaut-text.html
e. NASA space wear and living information
   http://spaceflight.nasa.gov/living/space wear/index.html
f. Space station
   http://www.nasa.gov/mission_pages/ station/main/index.html
g. Landings today
   http://www.nasa.gov/mission_pages/ station/structure/elements/soyuz/landing .html

II. Instructions
1. Lead a discussion of the things students noticed in the book that might be necessary for space travel and where the astronauts in the book went.
2. Write down the things and places the students noticed in the art. Record their responses where everyone can see them.
3. Tell the students they will be looking for ways the pictures and the words help you understand the book better in the next activity.

III. Procedure
Part 1
1. Page through the book and add the names of images not mentioned in the earlier discussion. Ask the students to notice the illustrations and find things that are not on the list.
2. Review each of the listed words to check for understanding as needed.
3. Choose a spread from the text with good imagery. (Suggestions: landing on the Moon, liftoff, or weightlessness in space.) Read the text from that spread.
4. Discuss how the pictures and text are related. Review the idea presented on the page and compare what the artist did. Look for the ideas presented in the pictures and how they add to the text. Point out how the pictures

2. Write informative/ explanatory texts to examine and convey complex ideas and information clearly and accurately through the effective selection, organization, and analysis of content.

3. Write narratives to develop real or imagined experiences or events using effective technique, well-chosen details, and well-structured event sequences.

Production and Distribution of Writing

4. Produce clear and coherent writing in which the development, organization, and style are appropriate to task, purpose, and audience.

5. Develop and strengthen writing as needed by planning, revising, editing, rewriting, or trying a new approach.

6. Use technology, including the Internet, to produce and publish writing and to interact and collaborate with others.

Research to Build and Present Knowledge

7. Conduct short as well as more sustained research projects based on focused questions, demonstrating understanding of the subject under investigation.

8. Gather relevant information from multiple print and digital sources, assess the credibility and accuracy of each source, and integrate the information while avoiding plagiarism.

9. Draw evidence from literary or informational texts to support analysis, reflection, and research.

Range of Writing

10. Write routinely over extended time frames (time for research, reflection, and revision) and shorter time frames (a single sitting or a day or two) for a range of tasks, purposes, and audiences.

Speaking and Listening Standards (5)

Comprehension and Collaboration

1. Prepare for and participate effectively in a range of conversations and collaborations with diverse partners, building on others' ideas and expressing their own clearly and persuasively.

2. Integrate and evaluate information presented in diverse media and formats, including visually, quantitatively, and orally.

Presentation of Knowledge and Ideas

4. Present information, findings, and supporting evidence such that listen-

show things not reflected by the words. For older students, include a writing activity to describe the art using figures of speech or other imagery.

5. Together, identify and state the main idea of the text. Then read the text on the spread with the splash down. Tell the students that this is how astronauts used to land. Ask what they think the author opened up for the illustrator to show by discussing the art on this spread.

6. Show how astronauts returned to Earth using the space shuttle and then how they land today as they return from the International Space Station by showing the Landings today site. Summarize the information as you show the site according to the grade level. (Landings today http://www.nasa.gov/mission_pages/station/structure/elements/soyuz/landing.html).

7. Then discuss the sensations the astronauts might feel during splash down. Remind the students that words and art work together to convey ideas.

8. Put three to five examples of then and now by listing them on the graphic organizer. You can do this as a large group, in small groups, or as individuals.

9. Have the students create their own page to accompany the book that will show both the early kind of landings and the current ways landings take place today. Ask them to divide their drawing paper in half and label it: Then and Now.

10. Write and describe the sensory details the astronauts might have experienced in the capsule as it fell and landed in the ocean.

11. On the opposite side of the page, repeat the activity, but use the way astronauts land today.

12. Illustrate their text in a manner similar to the book where both parts work to tell the story for both the Then and Now sides.

13. Lead a discussion about the essential question.

✎ *Suggested lesson break.*

Part 2

1. Tell the students that space travel has changed a great deal since the year 1969. Remind them of the first part of the lesson where they saw the two different kinds of landings (http://www.nasa.gov/mission_pages/station/structure/elements/soyuz/landing.html).

2. Show them selected pictures from the International Space Station. Ask them to look for the differences in astronauts now as compared to those in the early days that they saw in the book and point them out.
Tour by Suni Williams of ISS video (http://www.nasa.gov/mission_pages/station/main/suni_iss_tour.html).
For images, click on Missions, then choose past or current missions, and select ISS or Apollo to see them (http://www.nasa.gov/mission_pages/station/main/index.html).

3. Discuss what the students see as you move through the images and what differences they noticed between astronauts now and those in the space station. Point out the female astronaut and tell the students at first girls couldn't even become astronauts (http://www.nasa.gov/mission_pages/apollo/index.html; http://www.nasa.gov/multimedia/imagegallery/iotd.html).

4. Show the female astronauts using the gallery listed below. Use the images to notice differences and discuss the efforts of women wanting to enter the space program (http://womenshistory.about.com/od/aviationspace/ig/Women-Astronauts/). Point out the dates. Additional images from image gallery show more differences, especially 3, 9, and 40. (http://womenshistory.about.com/od/aviationspace/ig/Women-Astronauts/).

ers can follow the line of reasoning and the organization, development, and style are appropriate to task, purpose, and audience.

5. Make strategic use of digital media and visual displays of data to express information and enhance understanding of presentations.

6. Adapt speech to a variety of contexts and communicative tasks, demonstrating command of formal English when indicated or appropriate.

Language Standards (6)

Conventions of Standard English

1. Demonstrate command of the conventions of standard English grammar and usage when writing or speaking.

2. Demonstrate command of the conventions of standard English capitalization, punctuation, and spelling when writing.

Knowledge of Language

3. Apply knowledge of language to understand how language functions in different contexts, to make effective choices for meaning or style, and to comprehend more fully when reading or listening.

Vocabulary Acquisition and Use

4. Determine or clarify the meaning of unknown and multiple-meaning words and phrases by using context clues, analyzing meaningful word parts, and consulting general and specialized reference materials, as appropriate.

5. Demonstrate understanding of figurative language, word relationships, and nuances in word meanings.

6. Acquire and use accurately a range of general academic and domain-specific words and phrases sufficient for reading, writing, speaking, and listening at the college and career readiness level; demonstrate independence in gathering vocabulary knowledge when encountering an unknown term important to comprehension or expression.

Mathematical Practices (7)

1. Make sense of problems and persevere in solving them.

2. Reason abstractly and quantitatively.

3. Construct viable arguments and critique the reasoning of others.

4. Model with mathematics.

5. Present the information from the NASA website about what astronauts wear to conclude the lesson. Discuss the reasons for the sort of clothing and equipment needed in space. Compare the book pictures to the current images and notice the differences (http://www.nasa.gov/audience/for students/k-4/playandlearn/best-dressed -astronaut-text.html).

IV.　Reflect

1. Have the students talk to a partner about something they learned from the book.
2. Have the students place their drawings on their desks. Tell them to move around the room and look at the other pictures.
3. Have students return to their desks and look over their pictures. Have students think about one thing their pictures show.

V.　Assessment

Choice 1

Give the students an image from the earlier lesson. Have them write a sentence or paragraph about the picture and have them create their own image to support that sentence.

Choice 2

Write a few short statements that explain the differences in space travel and astronauts in the early days to how it is now. Write the explanation as a paragraph, bulleted lists, or in simple statement sentences. You could also use a Venn diagram for their information.

Collaborative Teacher Activity

History of Space Timeline

I.　Materials: space timeline resources (preselected, printed off and cut into sections); sentence strips (cut into smaller sections); pencils and markers

These websites will help you locate specific information as you go through the lesson:

a. Timeline resource
   http://www.spacekids.co.uk/space history/

b. Reference for additional information about the timeline
http://science.nationalgeographic.com/science/space/space-exploration-timeline/

c. Additional timeline resource
http://teacher.scholastic.com/space/space_firsts/index.htm

d. Apollo 11 story
http://teacher.scholastic.com/space/apollo11/index.htm

e. Astronaut bios
http://www.jsc.nasa.gov/Bios/astrobio.html

II. Instructions

1. Tell the class that they will be creating a classroom timeline to feature important dates in the history of space travel.

2. They will use the prepared information to read about their assigned date to identify and summarize the information and illustrate their writing in a manner similar to a picture book.

III. Activity

1. Pass out the sentence strips and individual pieces of the timeline. Double up if there are fewer than twenty-two students.

2. Allow the students enough time to read and then write their sentences on paper. Have them add the date that their event took place and write their two sentences on the sentence strip in pencil. Go over the information in markers.

3. Have them add art to the text to support their information.

🖉 *Suggested lesson break.*

4. Instruct the students to arrange their timeline in the correct order. Lay the sentence strips along the floor to order them. Then post the timeline around the classroom.

5. Have students read their section of the timeline and tell what pictures they drew to support their writing. Alternatively, you might

5. Use appropriate tools strategically.

6. Attend to precision.

7. Look for and make use of structure.

Mathematical Content (12)

Counting and Cardinality

- Know number names and the count sequence.
- Compare numbers.

Operations and Algebraic Thinking

- Use the four operations with whole numbers to solve problems.
- Write and interpret numerical expressions.
- Analyze patterns and relationships.

Number and Operations in Base Ten

- Generalize place value understanding for multi-digit whole numbers.
- Use place value understanding and properties of operations to perform multi-digit arithmetic.

Measurement and Data

- Describe and compare measurable attributes.
- Classify objects and count the number of objects in categories.
- Solve problems involving measurement and estimation of intervals of time, liquid volumes, and masses of objects.

- Convert like measurement units within a given measurement system.
- Represent and interpret data.

prefer that students make their presentations using a technology they can manage and present it in that form.

  IV. Reflection
1. Have the students move through the timeline, reading and looking at the pictures.
2. Tell them to return to their seats and write down what they liked about their part of the timeline and what they might do differently if they worked on another timeline again.

  V. Assessment

Choice 1

Use the student readings to ensure that they understood what they wrote and illustrated.

Choice 2

Have the students choose another space event from the timeline, read it and examine the art, and then write to explain that event in their own words.

Extension Activities

1. Read the following photo story about the Apollo 11 space mission to the students after reading the book. Project it so the images show as you read (http://teacher.scholastic.com/space/apollo11/index.htm).
2. Choose an astronaut from those listed on the NASA website (http://www.jsc.nasa.gov/Bios/astrobio.html).
   Have the students read about an astronaut and report on that person.
3. Look up additional information about the three astronauts from the book. Write down facts about each one and share with the class.
4. Teach a lesson on phases of the moon.
5. After reading the book, have the students write a short description of the main idea of the book. Use the phrase, "I am a technology specialist. I know that _____."

Modifications for Grades K–1

1. After reading the book, review the art. Use a specific spread to point out how the pictures tell the story, too.
2. Prepare and pass out to the students a page of text taken from the book without the pictures.
3. Have them illustrate the page to show how the art supports the words on a page.
4. Show them the images from part 2 of the library lesson and point out the space program's differences from the early days and now. Together, list two or three examples of the Then and Now and have students write them on the graphic organizer.

5. Then have the students choose a Then and Now topic and draw a picture to show one of the differences. (Suggested topics might include spacecraft that went to the moon and the International Space Station, men astronauts and women in the space program, short trip to space and living for a year at the ISS, water landing and landing on the ground in Russia.)

6. Have them fold their papers in half to divide it and label the two sides Then and Now.

7. For the timeline, you may want to adapt this activity to contain the date, a word or two, and art. The teacher may wish to read the text to each student or group.

Differentiation strategies:

1. Discuss, define, or review the vocabulary before or after reading the book.

2. Create the illustrations in a three-dimensional art form.

3. Have the students choose five important dates in the space program and explain why they chose those dates rather than making a class timeline.

4. Use strategic grouping by working in pairs or small groups to complete the activity.

5. Use a page of text from the book and ask the students to make their own interpretation of the art to support the text.

6. Use the images to keep a written record of the differences in space travel and give a copy to each student to use for the activities.

7. Allow the students to use technology to find the timeline information from the suggested sites and create their own timeline presentation as a class program.

8. Have the students write more for the comparison activities and then present their findings using some form of technology.

Resources:

Tour by Suni Williams of ISS
http://www.nasa.gov/mission_pages/station/main/suni_iss_tour.html

Additional images from image gallery show more differences, especially 3, 9, and 40.
http://www.nasa.gov/multimedia/imagegallery/iotd.html

Women astronauts and changes
http://womenshistory.about.com/od/aviationspace/ig/Women-Astronauts/

Astronaut clothing
http://www.nasa.gov/audience/forstudents/k-4/playandlearn/best-dressed
  -astronaut-text.html

NASA space wear and living information
http://spaceflight.nasa.gov/living/spacewear/index.html

Space station
http://www.nasa.gov/mission_pages/station/main/index.html

Landings today
http://www.nasa.gov/mission_pages/station/
  structure/elements/soyuz/landing.html

Index page to use to find images.
http://www.nasa.gov/mission_pages/station/main/index.html

Then and now images
http://www.nasa.gov/multimedia/imagegallery/iotd.html

Then and now Apollo images
http://www.nasa.gov/mission_pages/apollo/index.html

Female astronauts
http://womenshistory.about.com/od/aviationspace/ig/Women-Astronauts/

Timeline resource
http://www.spacekids.co.uk/spacehistory/

Reference for additional information about the timeline
http://science.nationalgeographic.com/science/space/space-exploration-timeline/

Additional timeline resource
http://teacher.scholastic.com/space/space_firsts/index.htm

Apollo 11 story
http://teacher.scholastic.com/space/apollo11/index.htm

Astronaut bios
http://www.jsc.nasa.gov/Bios/astrobio.html

Exemplar Texts:

Destined for Space: Our Story of Exploration.
By Don Nardo. Capstone, 2012. 64p. (9781429675406)
Grade Level: 2–6
ATOS Reading Level: 5.4
Lexile Level: NC 720L
Dewey: 629

Eight Days Gone.
By Linda McReynolds. Charlesbridge, 2012. 44p. (9781580893640)
Grade Level: K–2
Lexile Level: AD 280L
Dewey: 629.45

Look to the Stars.
By Buzz Aldrin. Putnam, 2009. 40p. (9780399247217)
Grade Level: 1–3
ATOS Reading Level: 7.2
Dewey: 629.409

Moonshot: The Flight of Apollo 11.
By Brian Floca. Atheneum, 2009. 48p. (9781416950462)
Grade Level: K–5
ATOS Reading Level: 4.8
Lexile Level: AD 990L
Dewey: 629.454

One Giant Leap.
By Robert Burleigh. Philomel, 2009. 40p. (9780399238833)
Grade Level: 1–5
ATOS Reading Level: 3.0
Lexile Level: 470L
Dewey: 629.454

13

Multimedia Artist and Animator

By Matt Mullins. Cherry Lake Publishing, 2011. 32p. (9781602799424)

Grade Level: 3–5 (*Grades K–2 with modifications*)
ATOS Reading Level: 4.9
Lexile Level: 690L
Dewey: 650.14
Subject Area: technology, art, writing

Essential Question: How can technology be used to create art?

Unit Summary: Students will examine the essential question, "How can technology be used to create art?" They will work as individuals or in pairs to explore using an image as their canvas and adding features that will become animated after completing their creation to their satisfaction. They will explain their choices by discussing them and then writing about them on a graphic organizer. They will then relate this activity to a job using art or animation. The students or pairs will save their work for the librarian to print.

Vocabulary: accelerates, bonded, circuit, contaminants, creatively, current, engineering, friction, innovations, latex, materials, molecules, pigments, properties, recyclable, results, solar, solutions, stabilize, thermal energy, vibration

Approximate lesson time: two class periods

Integration of Knowledge and Ideas

7. Integrate and evaluate content presented in diverse media and formats, including visually and quantitatively, as well as in words.

Range of Reading and Level of Text Complexity

10. Read and comprehend complex literary and informational texts independently and proficiently.

Writing Standards (9)

Text Types and Purposes

2. Write informative/explanatory texts to examine and convey complex ideas and information clearly and accurately through the effective selection, organization, and analysis of content.

3. Write narratives to develop real or imagined experiences or events using effective technique, well-chosen details, and well-structured event sequences.

Production and Distribution of Writing

4. Produce clear and coherent writing in which the development, organization, and style are appropriate to task, purpose, and audience.

5. Develop and strengthen writing as needed by planning, revising, editing, rewriting, or trying a new approach.

Booktalk: Have you heard of an artist or animator? You might be interested in these subjects if you've ever done an art activity and enjoyed it. But art isn't just painting, drawing, or coloring. Do you like reading graphic novels or comics? Maybe you've noticed signs, billboards, or other advertisements and wondered who designed them. Video games, computer icons, and logos are other ways artists and animators produce art. Sculpture is another kind of art. Let's look at the book *Multimedia Artist and Animator* to see what goes into becoming an artist or animator as your career.

Book Time

1. Share the booktalk for *Multimedia Artist and Animator* (above).
2. Read the book aloud, but skip the sidebars the first time through.
3. Return to the book and read the sidebars one at a time. Select a few sidebars to read and lead a discussion about the point it makes.

 Library Activity

Make Your Art Move!

I. Materials: computers (one per student or pairs), writing materials, graphic organizer
II. Instructions
    1. Tell the students they will be creating their own art and then see it animated. They will write about the art they created and explain their choices, so remind them to think about their choices as they make them or discuss them with their partner. Their writing will include the components they chose and the related placement of the extra images as well as discussing the completed image.
    2. Post the following URLs where everyone can see them. Tell them they can create an abstract picture with a ship on the water or one with faces and background. URLs: http://www.nga.gov/kids/zone/seasaws.htm or
    http://www.nga.gov/kids/zone/faces.htm

3. Instruct the students to type in the URL and go to the site.

4. Review some of the icons and tell the students to try out some of the available art.

III. Procedure

1. Have the students practice learning what each icon does and let them work with the features for a while. Remind them to try out each icon and examine the arrow button.

2. Allow time for the students to practice using the site.

3. Instruct everyone to erase their practice pictures.

✎ *Suggested lesson break.*

4. Students will next create their own art and then start the animation feature in order to watch their art animated.

5. Have them save their finished creation. Make sure their name is included in the file title. You will need to set up a file for each class involved.

6. Instruct the students to use the graphic organizer to respond to the questions about their art and why they made those choices. Remind them an artist makes specific choices and uses them to create a whole picture. They will use the questions as a guide to help them review their work as they write.

7. Discuss their writing thoughts and discuss the essential question.

IV. Reflect

1. Have the students return to their saved art image. Ask them to think why they chose the objects to include and why they placed them in that position and how they might make any changes if they could.

2. Let the students move around and view the art of the other students on the screens.

V. Assessment

Choice 1

Monitor the students as they work and view their finished product before they save their work.

6. Use technology, including the Internet, to produce and publish writing and to interact and collaborate with others.

Research to Build and Present Knowledge

7. Conduct short as well as more sustained research projects based on focused questions, demonstrating understanding of the subject under investigation.

8. Gather relevant information from multiple print and digital sources, assess the credibility and accuracy of each source, and integrate the information while avoiding plagiarism.

9. Draw evidence from literary or informational texts to support analysis, reflection, and research.

Range of Writing

10. Write routinely over extended time frames (time for research, reflection, and revision) and shorter time frames (a single sitting or a day or two) for a range of tasks, purposes, and audiences.

Speaking and Listening Standards (5)

Comprehension and Collaboration

1. Prepare for and participate effectively in a range of conversations and collaborations with diverse

partners, building on others' ideas and expressing their own clearly and persuasively.

2. Integrate and evaluate information presented in diverse media and formats, including visually, quantitatively, and orally.

Presentation of Knowledge and Ideas

4. Present information, findings, and supporting evidence such that listeners can follow the line of reasoning and the organization, development, and style are appropriate to task, purpose, and audience.

5. Make strategic use of digital media and visual displays of data to express information and enhance understanding of presentations.

6. Adapt speech to a variety of contexts and communicative tasks, demonstrating command of formal English when indicated or appropriate.

Language Standards (6)

Conventions of Standard English

1. Demonstrate command of the conventions of standard English grammar and usage when writing or speaking.

2. Demonstrate command of the conventions of standard English capital-

Choice 2
Review the printed art from each student.

 ## Collaborative Teacher Activity

Why Your Art Matters!

I. Materials: writing materials, computers
II. Instructions
    1. Tell the students they will write about their artistic process and create a short presentation on the computer to show this.
    2. Tell them they will plan their writing first.
    3. Have the students review their graphic organizers.
III. Activity
    1. Have the students look at their artwork, either online or the printed version.
    2. Each student will copy the saved image and paste it into a Word document.
    3. Save the page with a title.
    4. Each student will use the art they created and the graphic organizer notes to write two pages describing their artwork, the process, what they might like to change if they did the art again, and the feelings the finished product evoked.
    5. Save their art/description combination or print it when they finish.
IV. Reflection
    1. Have the students review their writing. Ask them to read it and see if it contains the kind of conventions good writing uses. Check for organization, content, and order.
V. Assessment
    Choice 1
    Have each student revise his or her own work for an evaluation by the teacher.
    Choice 2
    Turn in the first draft for review.

Extension Activities

1. Using the government site, have the students explore further in other areas to create different kinds of art.

2. Turn the art they created into a four panel comic and include text to go with it. See this website for a four panel comic template: http://donnayoung.org/art/comics.htm.

3. Use the printed art products and embellish them with other materials you have, such as cut paper, markers, crayons, map pencils, or paint. Write a comparison of the two different art pieces.

4. Have the students design a book cover that they might like their favorite book to have in place of the current one.

5. After reading the book, have the students write a short description of the main idea of the book. Use the phrase, "I am a technology specialist. I know that _____."

Modifications for Grades K–2

1. Select portions of the book to read to the students.
2. Discuss the word animation and how it relates to art.
3. Give the students examples within their own experiences and talk about how art is used there.
4. Show them a graphic novel.
5. Then move to the computers and show the URL.
6. Walk the students through the features on one image you choose until they can manage the site.
7. Have them work in pairs to make their picture.
8. Modify the graphic organizer to fit their abilities and have them describe their final picture by writing a few sentences or a paragraph about it.

Differentiation strategies:

1. Discuss, define, or review the vocabulary after reading the book. Point out examples of how the words were used.
2. Have the students keep their own notes about their thoughts and experiences rather than using the graphic organizers.
3. Practice manipulating the components on the site by walking the students through the process together the first time and indicating what each button does.

izization, punctuation, and spelling when writing.

Knowledge of Language

3. Apply knowledge of language to understand how language functions in different contexts, to make effective choices for meaning or style, and to comprehend more fully when reading or listening.

Vocabulary Acquisition and Use

4. Determine or clarify the meaning of unknown and multiple-meaning words and phrases by using context clues, analyzing meaningful word parts, and consulting general and specialized reference materials, as appropriate.

5. Demonstrate understanding of figurative language, word relationships, and nuances in word meanings.

6. Acquire and use accurately a range of general academic and domain-specific words and phrases sufficient for reading, writing, speaking, and listening at the college and career readiness level; demonstrate independence in gathering vocabulary knowledge when encountering an unknown term important to comprehension or expression.

Mathematical Practices (6)

1. Make sense of problems and persevere in solving them.

2. Reason abstractly and quantitatively.

3. Construct viable arguments and critique the reasoning of others.

5. Use appropriate tools strategically.

6. Attend to precision.

7. Look for and make use of structure.

Mathematical Content (23)

Counting and Cardinality

- Know number names and the count sequence.
- Count to tell the number of objects.
- Compare numbers.

Operations and Algebraic Thinking

- Understand addition as putting together and adding to, and understand subtraction as taking apart and taking from.
- Solve problems involving the four operations, and identify and explain patterns in arithmetic.
- Write and interpret numerical expressions.
- Analyze patterns and relationships.

Number and Operations in Base Ten

- Understand place value.
- Use place value understanding and properties

4. Have the students orally describe and explain their work to a partner, the teacher, the class, or have them record it.
5. Ask the students to choose a theme and create their images to correlate with that theme.
6. Have the students add images to their writing activity using technology or their own design.
7. Create a second picture and then have them write to explain the changes they used when creating the second picture.
8. Read the book in sections or choose two or three high-interest chapters to read aloud.
9. Make a list of the jobs related to art mentioned in the book and have that available for the students to use as a reference in their writing.

Resources:

Sea saws page with ship and background
http://www.nga.gov/kids/zone/seasaws.htm

Faces page with additions
http://www.nga.gov/kids/zone/faces.htm

Comic strip templates
http://donnayoung.org/art/comics.htm

Comic creator
http://www.readwritethink.org/files/resources/interactives/comic/

MakeBeliefsComix.com
http://www.makebeliefscomix.com/Comix/

Exemplar Texts:

Adventures in Cartooning.
By James Sturm. First Second, 2009. 112p.
  (9781596433694)
Grade Level: PreS–5
ATOS Reading Level: 2.1
Lexile Level: GN 170L
Dewey: 741.5

Art for Kids: Comic Strips: Create Your Own Comic Strips from Start to Finish.
By Art Roche. Sterling, 2011. 112p. (9781402784743)
Grade Level: 3–8
Lexile Level: IG 940L
Dewey: 741.5

Behind the Canvas: An Artist's Life.
By Blanca Apodaca and Michael Serwich. Teacher Created Materials, 2012. 48p. (9781433348266)
Grade Level: 3–6
ATOS Reading Level: 4.2
Lexile Level: 660L
Dewey: 650.14

Seeing Symmetry.
By Loreen Leedy. Holiday House, 2012. 32p. (9780823423606)
Grade Level: 2–4
Lexile Level: 640L
Dewey: 516.1

Setting Up the Shot.
By Jason Skog. Compass Point Books, 2012. 48p. (9780756545321)
Grade Level: 4–8
ATOS Reading Level: 5.4
Lexile Level: 840L
Dewey: 770

of operations to add and subtract.

Measurement and Data
- Describe and compare measurable attributes.
- Measure lengths indirectly and by iterating length units.
- Convert like measurement units within a given measurement system.
- Solve problems involving measurement and estimation of intervals of time, liquid volumes, and masses of objects.
- Represent and interpret data.
- Geometric measurement: understand concepts of area and relate area to multiplication and to addition.
- Geometric measurement: recognize perimeter as an attribute of plane figures and distinguish between linear and area measures.
- Geometric measurement: understand concepts of angle and measure angles.

Geometry
- Identify and describe shapes.
- Analyze, compare, create, and compose shapes.
- Reason with shapes and their attributes.
- Draw and identify lines and angles, and classify shapes by properties of their lines and angles.
- Classify two-dimensional figures into categories based on their properties.
- Geometric measurement: understand concepts of volume and relate volume to multiplication and to addition.

14

Wired

By Anastasia Suen. Charlesbridge, 2007. 32p. (9781570915994)

Grade Level: 3–5 *(Grades K–2 with modifications)*
ATOS Reading Level: 5.1
Lexile Level: 820L
Dewey: 621.3
Subject Area: science, language arts, art

Essential Question: Where does electricity come from?

Unit Summary: Students will examine the essential question, "Where does electricity come from?" As you read the book, the students will identify and write the main idea for each spread. They will look up generators and read about them. Using the library resources and on-line materials, they will create a diagram of a generator and label it. Finally, students will design a flow chart leading from the generator diagram of where electricity goes when it leave the generator and they'll use their collected information to write about the entire process.

Vocabulary: appliances, breaker, cables, coil, electrician, electricity, feeder lines, generator, grounding rod, magnetic field, substation, transformer, transmission, voltage

Approximate lesson time: one to two class periods

Booktalk: Scuff your feet across the carpet in winter and touch a doorknob. What happens? Often you might feel a shock or see a tiny spark fly from your finger. That was a tiny current of electricity. You build up static

and figurative meanings, and analyze how specific word choices shape meaning or tone.

5. Analyze the structure of texts, including how specific sentences, paragraphs, and larger portions of the text (e.g., a section, chapter, scene, or stanza) relate to each other and the whole.

6. Assess how point of view or purpose shapes the content and style of a text.

Integration of Knowledge and Ideas

7. Integrate and evaluate content presented in diverse media and formats, including visually and quantitatively, as well as in words.

Range of Reading and Level of Text Complexity

10. Read and comprehend complex literary and informational texts independently and proficiently.

Writing Standards (10)

Text Types and Purposes

1. Write arguments to support claims in an analysis of substantive topics or texts, using valid reasoning and relevant and sufficient evidence.

2. Write informative/ explanatory texts to examine and convey

electricity that passes from your body to the metal doorknob. We use electricity every day. Lights, televisions, computers, vacuum cleaners, and toasters are just a few of the things that use electricity. But that tiny spark doesn't pack enough power to provide the electricity we use every day. How do we get this power? What makes electricity? How does it get to our homes? Let's find out by reading the book *Wired.*

Book Time

1. Share the booktalk for *Wired* (above).
2. Read the bolded poem from the book through the first time without showing the pictures or reading the main text.
3. Return to the first page and ask the students what they think the book is about. Return to the poem, still not showing the pictures, and lead a discussion about what the poetry might mean. You might want to use two pages of poetry at a time.
4. Then read the book through, reminding the students of the poem. Show the art as you read.

 ## Library Activity

Technology and Electricity

I.   Materials: *Wired,* any resources about generators, online materials, writing materials, small drawing paper, graphic organizer
II. Instructions
1. Tell the students they will be identifying the main idea from each spread of the book as you reread the book and then take a look at how electricity comes from generators.
2. You'll discuss the spreads together, and they will write down the main idea after the discussion.
3. They will explore generators and make a diagram of one.
4. Later, they'll use their collected information to create a flow chart to illustrate how electricity is generated and how it moves from the generator to the house.

III. Procedure
  1. Read the book again. At each spread, stop and discuss the main idea on the two pages.
  2. After the discussion, each student will write it down in list form on the graphic organizer.
  3. Complete the book and notes list.

✐ *Suggested lesson break.*

  4. For the next part, the students will explore how a generator works.
  5. They will make a diagram of a generator and label the parts after reading more about them.
  6. They will begin by looking at an explanation of generators. This site will show an example of a generator and its parts: http://ga.water.usgs.gov/edu/hyhowworks.html.
     This site explains how water turns a generator: http://www.eia.gov/kids/energy.cfm?page=hydropower_home-basics.
  7. Students will diagram a generator with labels. They will next make a flow chart to show where the electricity goes once it leaves the generator. They can use their notes and short phrases to make the chart. Have them title their diagram and flow chart.
  8. Next, have the students write a several-paragraph description of a generator and how it works or write about how electricity flows from generators through our homes using the information they have collected.
  9. Discuss the essential question and relate it to generators.
IV. Reflect
  1. Ask the students to exchange their writing and read them silently.
  2. Then have them return the papers and reread their own work.
  3. Give them the opportunity to make any changes.
V. Assessment
  Choice 1
     Read the student papers to make sure they covered the main parts of a generator in their writing or how electricity moves from a generator to their homes.

complex ideas and information clearly and accurately through the effective selection, organization, and analysis of content.

3. Write narratives to develop real or imagined experiences or events using effective technique, well-chosen details, and well-structured event sequences.

Production and Distribution of Writing

4. Produce clear and coherent writing in which the development, organization, and style are appropriate to task, purpose, and audience.

5. Develop and strengthen writing as needed by planning, revising, editing, rewriting, or trying a new approach.

6. Use technology, including the Internet, to produce and publish writing and to interact and collaborate with others.

Research to Build and Present Knowledge

7. Conduct short as well as more sustained research projects based on focused questions, demonstrating understanding of the subject under investigation.

8. Gather relevant information from multiple print and digital sources, assess the credibility and accu-

racy of each source, and integrate the information while avoiding plagiarism.

9. Draw evidence from literary or informational texts to support analysis, reflection, and research.

Range of Writing

10. Write routinely over extended time frames (time for research, reflection, and revision) and shorter time frames (a single sitting or a day or two) for a range of tasks, purposes, and audiences.

Speaking and Listening Standards (6)

Comprehension and Collaboration

1. Prepare for and participate effectively in a range of conversations and collaborations with diverse partners, building on others' ideas and expressing their own clearly and persuasively.

2. Integrate and evaluate information presented in diverse media and formats, including visually, quantitatively, and orally.

3. Evaluate a speaker's point of view, reasoning, and use of evidence and rhetoric.

Presentation of Knowledge and Ideas

4. Present information, findings, and supporting

Choice 2

Have the students identify and explain five to ten words relating to electricity and how it is generated and moves to peoples' homes.

Collaborative Teacher Activity

Electric Words!

I. Materials: class set of dictionaries, writing materials, vocabulary list
II. Instructions
1. Explain that Benjamin Franklin not only invented the lightning rod, but many other things as well, like bifocal eyeglasses, the Franklin stove, the odometer, and swim fins. He used his talents in many ways. As he worked on his explanation about electricity, he wrote in a letter: "I feel a Want of Terms here and doubt much whether I shall be able to make this intelligible."

    So not only did Franklin have to explain his theories, he also had to make up words to describe them. Among them were these terms related to electricity: armature, battery, charge, condenser, conductor, plus, minus, positively, and negatively.
2. Tell the students that they will look up these words in the dictionary and explain their relationship to electricity in two to three sentences. You can have them work in groups or individually.
3. Then tell them before they do the activity, you'll read the book. As you read, they should look for five more words to add to their list. They may use any word related to electricity that was used in the book. Tell them that they might want to write down more than five words and then they can choose the five they like from their own list.
III. Activity
1. Read the book to the class. Point out a few possible suggestions for inclusion into their vocabulary lesson as you read.

2. Allow the students time to look up their words and write about the relationship each word has to electricity.

🖉 *Suggested lesson break.*

3. Ask the students to create a poster showing the words and post them around the room.

IV. Reflection

1. Ask the students to read over their own definitions and think about each one. Decide if they understand the meaning for each word.

2. Have them pair up and read their sentence writing from three of their definitions. Ask them to make sure that both people understand their meaning.

3. End their vocabulary activity by having them write in one sentence that states the main idea of *Wired*.

V. Assessment

Choice 1

Read the sentences that accompany the definitions the students wrote to see if they comprehended the meaning of their words.

Choice 2

Have the students write down five to seven facts about how electricity moves from the generator to peoples' homes.

Extension Activities

1. Write an original poem that illustrates how electricity moves from a generator to peoples' homes.

2. Research some of the other inventions developed by Benjamin Franklin.

3. Explore other ways electricity is generated. Consider hydropower, solar power, tidal power, and wind power.

4. Look up some of the early scientists who studied electricity in some form. You may want to start with Benjamin Franklin, Thales of Miletus, William Gilbert, Otto von Guericke, Robert Boyle, Stephen Gray, Charles Francois du Fay,

evidence such that listeners can follow the line of reasoning and the organization, development, and style are appropriate to task, purpose, and audience.

5. Make strategic use of digital media and visual displays of data to express information and enhance understanding of presentations.

6. Adapt speech to a variety of contexts and communicative tasks, demonstrating command of formal English when indicated or appropriate.

Language Standards (6)

Conventions of Standard English

1. Demonstrate command of the conventions of standard English grammar and usage when writing or speaking.

2. Demonstrate command of the conventions of standard English capitalization, punctuation, and spelling when writing.

Knowledge of Language

3. Apply knowledge of language to understand how language functions in different contexts, to make effective choices for meaning or style, and to comprehend more fully when reading or listening.

Vocabulary Acquisition and Use

4. Determine or clarify the meaning of unknown and multiple-meaning words and phrases by using context clues, analyzing meaningful word parts, and consulting general and specialized reference materials, as appropriate.

5. Demonstrate understanding of figurative language, word relationships, and nuances in word meanings.

6. Acquire and use accurately a range of general academic and domain-specific words and phrases sufficient for reading, writing, speaking, and listening at the college and career readiness level; demonstrate independence in gathering vocabulary knowledge when encountering an unknown term important to comprehension or expression.

Mathematical Practices (8)

1. Make sense of problems and persevere in solving them.

2. Reason abstractly and quantitatively.

3. Construct viable arguments and critique the reasoning of others.

4. Model with mathematics.

Ebenezer Kinnersley, Pieter van Musschenbroek, William Watson, Michael Faraday, Henry Cavendish, Coulomb of France, Luigi Galvani, Girolamo Cardano, Allesandro Volta, Thomas Edison, and Nicola Tesla. Explain the contribution of each person to electricity.

4. Bring in a guest speaker from the local power company.

5. Find out from what source the electricity used in your school is generated.

6. After reading the book, have the students write a short description of the main idea of the book. Use the phrase, "I am a technology specialist. I know that _____."

Modifications for Grades K–2

1. Read the poem and use it to explain the text in simple terms based on the information.
2. Discuss how electricity moves through the wires and into our homes.
3. Create a simple diagram with the students showing the completion of a circuit from generator to a home. Add appropriate words.
4. Review safety with the students by reading the final page.
5. Group the students and have each group make a picture or poster of the rule and illustrate it to show safety around electricity.
6. Have each group present their rule and tell why it is important.

Differentiation strategies:

1. Discuss, define, or review the vocabulary after reading the book. Point out examples of how the words were used.
2. Rather than writing about the process at the end of the activity, ask them to simply label their flow chart.
3. Have the students present their information orally.
4. Ask the students to find a different way to present the information they have learned.

5. Use strategic grouping and have them turn in a group product.
6. Create a 3-D model of a generator and label its parts.
7. Prepare the main idea notes ahead of time and give them to the students to follow as you read.
8. Work in groups to write the main idea or discuss it only.

Resources:

How hydroelectric power works
http://ga.water.usgs.gov/edu/hyhowworks.html

Hydropower for generating electricity
http://www.eia.gov/kids/energy
 .cfm?page=hydropower_home-basics

Description of a generator
http://ga.water.usgs.gov/edu/hyturbine.html

Exemplar Texts:

Electricity All Around.
By Barbara Alpert. Capstone Press, 2012. 24p.
 (9781596433694)
Grade Level: PreK–1
Lexile Level: 660L
Dewey: 621

Electricity.
By Felicia Law. Gareth Stevens, 2009. 32p.
 (9781433900310)
Grade Level: 2–5
ATOS Reading Level: 5.6
Lexile Level: IG 870L
Dewey: 537

Electricity.
By Matt Mullins. Childrens Press, 2012. 48p.
 (9780531263198)
Grade Level: 2–5
ATOS Reading Level: 5.2
Lexile Level: 740L
Dewey: 537

5. Use appropriate tools strategically.

6. Attend to precision.

7. Look for and make use of structure.

8. Look for and express regularity in repeated reasoning.

Mathematical Content (17)

Counting and Cardinality
- Know number names and the count sequence.
- Count to tell the number of objects.
- Compare numbers.

Operations and Algebraic Thinking
- Understand addition as putting together and adding to, and understand subtraction as taking apart and taking from.

Operations and Algebraic Thinking
- Understand properties of multiplication and the relationship between multiplication and division.
- Use the four operations with whole numbers to solve problems.
- Gain familiarity with factors and multiples.
- Generate and analyze patterns.

Number and Operations in Base Ten

- Generalize place value understanding for multi-digit whole numbers.
- Use place value understanding and properties of operations to perform multi-digit arithmetic.

Measurement and Data

- Describe and compare measurable attributes.
- Classify objects and count the number of objects in categories.
- Measure and estimate lengths in standard units.
- Represent and interpret data.
- Tell and write time.

Geometry

- Identify and describe shapes.
- Analyze, compare, create, and compose shapes.

How Electricity Works.
By Jennifer Swanson. Child's World, 2012. 32p. (9781609732165)
Grade Level: 2–5
ATOS Reading Level: 4.7
Dewey: 537

Using Electricity.
By Chris Oxlade. Heinemann, 2012. 32p. (9781432956769)
Grade Level: 1–3
ATOS Reading Level: 4.5
Dewey: 621

PART IV

Teaching Engineering in Your Library

Engineering is . . .

Definition: An engineer is a person who searches for and develops a product with a practical application to commerce or industry.

Background

Engineers look for solutions to problems after they've identified a specific need. They use a set of steps to identify the problem, decide who needs it, and explain why it is needed. These steps allow them to go through the process in order to find a solution to the identified problem by creating new products, systems, experiences, or environments.

As engineers work to solve the identified problem, they may move through the steps out of order and return to earlier steps. Working this way is called iteration. The first step includes defining the problem. Engineers ask: what is the need, who has this need, and should it be solved?

The second step involves research. They must know if there are people interested in using a product if it is developed, and they need to learn if there is already a solution that would address the problem.

The third step names the characteristics their solution has to meet to be successful. They often look at a similar product to find these key elements.

The fourth step is to come up with as many ideas for the solution as possible. Thinking of many solutions keeps them from looking at only one possible answer to the problem when another idea might work better. The greater the number of solutions they can think of, the better chance they have of finding the best solution.

The fifth step is to revise or improve their chosen solution method. Refining their ideas improves the product they intend to develop, and these ideas often go on throughout the design.

The sixth step involves building the first, working version of the solution. The engineer can then test this model to see how it will work. They may use different materials in the final version.

The seventh step is to test the product and then redesign it. With each test, problems emerge and the engineer makes changes to correct the problem. It may take a series of tests and changes to find the final, best design.

The last step is to let others know about what the engineer has designed. They communicate this in a report or as a display. They show their work and how they solved the problem so the new product can be made and used.

Students can follow these same steps if they wish to invent or design a product themselves.

15

Amazing Amusement Park Rides

By Meish Goldish. Bearport, 2012. 24p. (9781617723049)

Grade Level: 3–5 *(Grades K–2 with modifications)*
ATOS Reading Level: 4.9
Lexile Level: IG 880L (Illustrated Guide)
Dewey: 791.068
Subject Area: engineering, mathematics, writing

Essential Question: What information is needed to design a roller coaster?

Unit Summary: Students will examine the essential question, "What information is needed to design a roller coaster?" They will write down the statistics of the Steel Dragon coaster and then add their own statistics about a roller coaster they will design on the graphic organizer. Using the statistics, they will design and draw a roller-coaster track and car as a prototype for an amusement park ride lasting two to three minutes. They will plan first on paper and decide on their statistics, which they will put on their graphic organizer. Then they will transfer their design ideas to the large drawing paper and label all the required statistics. Students will share their roller coaster designs with the class.

Vocabulary: amusement park, attractions, coasters, crypt, geysers, gondola, height, hovers, length, lengthy, pace, size, spectacular, weight, winding

Approximate lesson time: two to three class periods

Common Core State Standards (41 total)

Reading Standards (5)

Key Ideas and Details

1. Read closely to determine what the text says explicitly and to make logical inferences from it; cite specific textual evidence when writing or speaking to support conclusions drawn from the text.

2. Determine central ideas or themes of a text and analyze their development; summarize the key supporting details and ideas.

3. Analyze how and why individuals, events, and ideas develop and interact over the course of a text.

Integration of Knowledge and Ideas

7. Integrate and evaluate content presented in diverse media and formats, including visually and quantitatively, as well as in words.

Range of Reading and Level of Text Complexity

10. Read and comprehend complex literary and informational texts independently and proficiently.

Writing Standards (9)

Text Types and Purposes

2. Write informative/explanatory texts to examine and convey complex ideas and information clearly and accurately through the effective selection, organization, and analysis of content.

3. Write narratives to develop real or imagined experiences or events using effective technique, well-chosen details, and well-structured event sequences.

Production and Distribution of Writing

4. Produce clear and coherent writing in which the development, organization, and style are appropriate to task, purpose, and audience.

5. Develop and strengthen writing as needed by planning, revising, editing, rewriting, or trying a new approach.

Booktalk: You've probably been to an amusement park. Can you remember the feeling in your stomach when you hurtled down the first breath-taking slope? Were your hands in the air or did you scream? Exciting amusement park rides don't simply appear from nowhere. Someone has to plan, design, and build them. That's the job of an engineer. Let's read about a couple of these rides and find out more about them. Take a look at the book *Amazing Amusement Park Rides*.

Book Time

1. Share the booktalk for *Amazing Amusement Park Rides* (above). Read the introductory section and then the chapters from the book for "Steel Dragon 2000" (p. 6–7) and "The Crypt"(p. 16–17) to the students.
2. Return to the "Steel Dragon 2000" section and identify all the statistics given for the roller coaster. Have the students write down the numbers on the graphic organizer to use as a basis for their assignment to come.
3. Review the statistics for "The Crypt" section as a comparison ride.
4. Show the students examples of roller coasters from this site: http://rollercoasterknowhow.webs.com/typesofrollercoasters.htm.
5. Discuss the different features.

✎ *Suggested lesson break.*

 Library Activity

Name That Coaster!

I.   Materials: notebook paper, pencils, rulers and yardsticks, map pencils, manila or large drawing paper, graphic organizer
II. Instructions
  1. Tell the students that they will design and draw a roller coaster track and the train that will be used with it. They will also name their roller coaster ride and put their roller coaster statistics on the graphic organizer.

2. Students will design a two- or three-minute roller coaster track and the train, and determine both the route and direction of the track, including the heights of the three tallest points.

III. Procedure
1. Tell the students to work individually.
2. Show them the picture of the tracks of the Steel Dragon on page 6.
3. Remind them they will be designing and drawing the roller coaster train as well. They need to indicate how many people can sit in each seat of the train so they can tell the number of people it can hold in one ride.
4. Tell them to include all their dimensions on their work, including all important heights, lengths of the track, and the train dimensions. The train cars should reflect the sizes and number of people it holds.
5. Suggest that the students make a plan on notebook paper and put their dimensions on it first. Then they will transfer their design to the large paper.

✏ *Suggested lesson break.*

6. Give the students time to design and draw their track and roller coaster train. Remind them to label their dimensions.
7. At the end of class, inform the students that they will use their information in another class and collect the papers to pass along to the collaborating teacher.
8. Lead a discussion about the successes and challenges of this assignment. Ask them to talk about how engineering might play a role in designing roller coasters and answer the essential question.

V. Reflect
1. Have the students pair/share about any parts of the design they had to change.
2. Then pair/share the name of their roller coaster.
3. Ask for volunteers to tell the name of their coasters and explain why they chose that name.

6. Use technology, including the Internet, to produce and publish writing and to interact and collaborate with others.

Research to Build and Present Knowledge

7. Conduct short as well as more sustained research projects based on focused questions, demonstrating understanding of the subject under investigation.

8. Gather relevant information from multiple print and digital sources, assess the credibility and accuracy of each source, and integrate the information while avoiding plagiarism.

9. Draw evidence from literary or informational texts to support analysis, reflection, and research.

Range of Writing

10. Write routinely over extended time frames (time for research, reflection, and revision) and shorter time frames (a single sitting or a day or two) for a range of tasks, purposes, and audiences.

Speaking and Listening Standards (4)

Comprehension and Collaboration

2. Integrate and evaluate information presented in diverse media and formats, including visu-

ally, quantitatively, and orally.

Presentation of Knowledge and Ideas

4. Present information, findings, and supporting evidence such that listeners can follow the line of reasoning and the organization, development, and style are appropriate to task, purpose, and audience.

5. Make strategic use of digital media and visual displays of data to express information and enhance understanding of presentations.

6. Adapt speech to a variety of contexts and communicative tasks, demonstrating command of formal English when indicated or appropriate.

Language Standards (4)

Conventions of Standard English

1. Demonstrate command of the conventions of standard English grammar and usage when writing or speaking.

2. Demonstrate command of the conventions of standard English capitalization, punctuation, and spelling when writing.

Knowledge of Language

3. Apply knowledge of language to understand

VI. Assessment
Choice 1
Use the student papers to assess their work.
Choice 2
Have the students write about their design. They should include a section on naming, challenges in the design, explanation of the design, and the sort of train that they designed. They should also include reasons why their roller coaster would be a fun ride to include in an amusement park.

⚙ Collaborative Teacher Activity

How Much Money Can I Make?

I. Materials: paper, pencils, roller coaster designs from the library lesson
II. Instructions
1. Tell the students they will be using their roller coaster designs to make some money today.
2. They won't actually make money, but they will calculate how many people can ride their coaster in an hour and use that information to calculate other figures necessary to running a profitable fair or amusement park ride.
III. Activity
1. Tell the students that every coaster will have three cars. Ask them to review how long their coaster ride takes. The rides should be either two or three minutes long. Review how to figure the number of trips in an hour the ride could take (if the coasters were staggered so that there was little or no wait time) and the cars were evenly spaced.
2. Tell them they'll be calculating as if the ride were busy and fully loaded on each trip that day.
3. Next, ask them to count the number of riders per coaster train.
4. Discuss and agree on a money figure for one roller coaster ride. Ask the class to use their personal experience to tell how they

should charge per ride. Agree on and then set the hours the amusement park will be open.

5. Note the following that each student is to figure out for his or her own roller coaster and mark on the back of the library graphic organizer:

Number of trips per hour
Number of riders per trip
Number of riders per hour
Collected money per one trip
Collected money per hour
Collected money for the day

6. Give the students time to work on their calculations.

7. When they finish, tell them that next they'll figure out how much money they'd make if the ride were only half full on every trip.

8. Follow the same list to calculate the figures for half the number of riders.

IV.   Reflect

1. Move the students into small groups. Ask them to exchange papers and review the figures and process their group mates used. Discuss the results.

2. Have the students look over their work to make sure everyone followed the correct process.

V.   Assessment

Choice 1

Check the student figures for their roller coaster work.

Choice 2

Assign your own set of information and have the students calculate part or all of the information they did during the assignment.

Extension Activities

1. Look up information about the history of roller coasters. Read and report on the ways roller coasters have changed since they began.

2. Look at pages 16–17 from the book. Use "The Crypt" ride to calculate the money that could be brought in for that ride using the assignment's requirements, times, and fees.

how language functions in different contexts, to make effective choices for meaning or style, and to comprehend more fully when reading or listening.

Vocabulary Acquisition and Use

6. Acquire and use accurately a range of general academic and domain-specific words and phrases sufficient for reading, writing, speaking, and listening at the college and career readiness level; demonstrate independence in gathering vocabulary knowledge when encountering an unknown term important to comprehension or expression.

Mathematical Practices (7)

1. Make sense of problems and persevere in solving them.

2. Reason abstractly and quantitatively.

3. Construct viable arguments and critique the reasoning of others.

4. Model with mathematics.

5. Use appropriate tools strategically.

6. Attend to precision.

7. Look for and make use of structure.

Mathematical Content (12)

Operations and Algebraic Thinking

- Represent and solve problems involving multiplication and division.
- Write and interpret numerical expressions.
- Analyze patterns and relationships.

Number and Operations in Base Ten

- Understand the place value system.
- Perform operations with multi-digit whole numbers and with decimals to hundredths.

Measurement and Data

- Measure and estimate lengths in standard units.
- Convert like measurement units within a given measurement system.
- Relate addition and subtraction to length.
- Work with time and money.
- Represent and interpret data.
- Geometric measurement: understand concepts of angle and measure angles.

Geometry

- Reason with shapes and their attributes.

3. Have students write a personal experience story about one of their favorite roller coasters.
4. Have the students add part features around their roller coasters.
5. After reading the book, have the students write a short description of the main idea of the book. Use the phrase, "I am an engineer. I know that _____."

Modifications for Grades K–2

1. Begin the lesson by viewing the images of different kinds of roller coasters.
2. Use one of the interactive sites to build and test a roller coaster in small groups. The first listed site is a fun one to build and it comments on the design. Have them name their roller coaster.
3. Have the students draw their coaster design from the computer screen.
4. Ask the students to repeat the activity, but make a boring ride and compare the two.
5. Have them draw a roller coaster car and indicate how many people it can hold in its seat. Have them figure out how many people could ride in two cars, three cars, and so on.
6. Instruct the students to write two story problems using their roller coaster cars.

Differentiation strategies:

1. Discuss, define, or review pertinent vocabulary and scientific principles of the assignment after reading the book.
2. Use strategic grouping for the activity.
3. Have the students work in groups to design the roller coasters.
4. Have the students look up and add the metric equivalents of their statistics.
5. Prepare a set of images that show more than one example of the different kinds of roller coasters there are.
6. Use one of the interactive design sites to build and test a roller coaster.
7. After using the interactive site, have the students design their own cars to figure the fees.

Resources:

Build your own roller coaster
http://kids.discovery.com/games/build-play/build-a-coaster

An interactive roller coaster design page
http://www.learner.org/interactives/parkphysics/coaster/

Another interactive roller coaster design page
http://puzzling.caret.cam.ac.uk/game.php?game=roller

Examples of the different kinds of roller coasters
http://rollercoasterknowhow.webs.com/typesofrollercoasters.htm

Choose roller coasters from this site for the students to view (includes statistics)
http://www.ultimaterollercoaster.com/coasters/pictures/

Exemplar Texts:

BIG Roller Coasters.
By Catherine Ipcizade. Capstone, 2010. 24p. (9781429633154)
Grade Level: PreK–2
ATOS Reading Level: 2.3
Lexile Level: 680L
Dewey: 791.068

Gravity in Action: Roller Coasters!
By Joan Newton. PowerKids Press, 2009. 24p. (9781435829763)
Grade Level: 3–5
ATOS Reading Level: 4.1
Dewey: 531.1

Heart-stopping Roller Coasters.
By Meish Goldish. Bearport, 2010. 24p. (9781597169561)
Grade Level: 3–5
ATOS Reading Level: 3.7
Lexile Level: 870L
Dewey: 791.068

Models and Designs: It's a Roller Coaster Ride!
By Emily Sohn and Anya Hansen. Norwood House Press, 2011. 48p. (9781599534299)
Grade Level: 4–6
ATOS Reading Level: 4.7
Lexile Level: 690L
Dewey: 609

Perimeter and Area at the Amusement Park.
By Dianne Irving. Capstone, 2011. 32p. (9781429666152)
Grade Level: 4–6
ATOS Reading Level: 4.4
Lexile Level: IG 730L
Dewey: 725.76

16

Build It! Invent New Structures and Contraptions

By Tammy Enz. Capstone Press, 2012. 32p. (9781429676359)

Grade Level: 3–5 *(Grades K–2 with modifications)*
Guided Reading Level: Q
Lexile Level: IG 740L (Illustrated Guide)
Dewey: 621
Subject Area: engineering, science, writing

Essential Question: What keeps a bridge from falling down?

Unit Summary: Students will examine the essential question, "What keeps a bridge from falling down?" In groups, students will search for and locate information related to the four major kinds of bridge supports—beams, arches, trusses, and suspension. They will complete a graphic organizer to explain how each of the four supports work to hold up bridges. Then they will use toothpicks or Popsicle sticks to practice forming arches or trusses and use that knowledge to plan and draw a design for a bridge of their own for their group.

Vocabulary: arches, beams, connections, design, principle, structures, suspension, toothpicks, truss, wedge

Approximate lesson time: one to two class periods

Common Core State Standards (47 total)

Reading Standards (6)

Key Ideas and Details

1. Read closely to determine what the text says explicitly and to make logical inferences from it; cite specific textual evidence when writing or speaking to support conclusions drawn from the text.

2. Determine central ideas or themes of a text and analyze their development; summarize the key supporting details and ideas.

Craft and Structure

4. Interpret words and phrases as they are used in a text, including determining technical, connotative, and figurative meanings, and analyze how specific word choices shape meaning or tone.

Integration of Knowledge and Ideas

7. Integrate and evaluate content presented in diverse media and formats, including visually and quantitatively, as well as in words.

8. Delineate and evaluate the argument and specific claims in a text, including the validity of the reasoning as well as the relevance and sufficiency of the evidence.

Range of Reading and Level of Text Complexity

10. Read and comprehend complex literary and informational texts independently and proficiently.

Writing Standards (8)

Text Types and Purposes

2. Write informative/ explanatory texts to examine and convey complex ideas and information clearly and accurately through the effective selection, organization, and analysis of content.

Production and Distribution of Writing

4. Produce clear and coherent writing in which

Booktalk: You could be the next Thomas Edison, Benjamin Franklin, or Ruth Wakefield. Who? What did Ruth Wakefield do? You may have tasted her invention—the chocolate chip cookie. Without her, you might never have tasted those delicious cookies. All of these people were inventors, and they worked like engineers. They came across a problem and looked for a solution. Sometimes what they learned came from a failure. Today we'll look at how engineers work and see the steps in practice. Let's take a look at the book *Build It*.

Book Time

1. Share the booktalk for *Build It* (above).
2. Read the introductory section on pages 4 and 5.
3. Review the Six Steps of Inventing from the engineering section at the start of the engineering lessons.
4. Then read the Coin Sorter Invention aloud on pages 16 to 19.
5. Discuss the ways the coin sorter models the steps engineers and inventors work.

✎ *Suggested lesson break.*

 Library Activity

Reinventing the Bridge

I. Materials: paper, pencils, graphic organizer for the Six Steps of Inventing, glue (either craft glue or a cool glue gun), box of toothpicks per group or package of Popsicle sticks per group (from craft store), graphic organizer

II. Instructions
1. Tell the students that today they will be identifying the problem, learning the principle for their problem, finding some ideas, and doing the planning for their bridge support design.
2. They will be learning about bridge supports and planning to design a bridge. Tell them that building a structure across the water requires some kind of support. They will be searching for the different kinds of

bridges and working to design a model bridge of their own that they will make in another class.

III. Procedure
   1. Divide the students into four or five groups.
   2. Tell the groups they will be searching for the ways bridges are supported. They will be looking for BATS—and not the mammal. Tell them that as a group they will come up with the names and kinds of supports used by engineers to support bridges. You may direct them to a specific website or let them explore. They should find beams, arches, trusses, or suspension (BATS).
   3. The students will write down each one and a two- or three-sentence explanation of each of the four supports named.
   4. Have the groups report back so that everyone is familiar with and has an example of each of the kinds of supports.

🖉 *Suggested lesson break.*

   5. Tell the students that you'll read the introduction to the toothpick bridge. After that, they will have some time to plan their bridges. They'll do the actual building with the collaborating teacher. They can choose to do an arch bridge with toothpicks or a truss bridge with Popsicle sticks.
   6. Read page 28 and show them the picture.
   7. Give the groups their box of toothpicks or sticks and let them begin their plans. Have them try different combinations to see what they might find for a structure plan. They may want to refer back to their research information.
   8. Ask each group to sketch their designs and the shape of the bridge they intend to make. They might want to do this on graph paper. Ask them to predict the number of toothpicks or sticks they will need to complete their bridge. Keep those sketches to use with the collaborating teacher when they'll build their bridge. Don't do the gluing yet, but allow

the development, organization, and style are appropriate to task, purpose, and audience.

5. Develop and strengthen writing as needed by planning, revising, editing, rewriting, or trying a new approach.

6. Use technology, including the Internet, to produce and publish writing and to interact and collaborate with others.

Research to Build and Present Knowledge

7. Conduct short as well as more sustained research projects based on focused questions, demonstrating understanding of the subject under investigation.

8. Gather relevant information from multiple print and digital sources, assess the credibility and accuracy of each source, and integrate the information while avoiding plagiarism.

9. Draw evidence from literary or informational texts to support analysis, reflection, and research.

Range of Writing

10. Write routinely over extended time frames (time for research, reflection, and revision) and shorter time frames (a single sitting or a day or two) for a range of tasks, purposes, and audiences.

Speaking and Listening Standards (6)

Comprehension and Collaboration

1. Prepare for and participate effectively in a range of conversations and collaborations with diverse partners, building on others' ideas and expressing their own clearly and persuasively.

2. Integrate and evaluate information presented in diverse media and formats, including visually, quantitatively, and orally.

Presentation of Knowledge and Ideas

4. Present information, findings, and supporting evidence such that listeners can follow the line of reasoning and the organization, development, and style are appropriate to task, purpose, and audience.

5. Make strategic use of digital media and visual displays of data to express information and enhance understanding of presentations.

6. Adapt speech to a variety of contexts and communicative tasks, demonstrating command of formal English when indicated or appropriate.

them to manipulate the sticks so they get an idea.
   9. Have each group show their final bridge design and tell why they chose that style and then discuss the essential question.
V.   Reflect
   1. Give the groups a few minutes to discuss what they've heard from the other groups.
   2. Have them look over their bridge design.
VI.   Assessment
   Choice 1
      Have the students individually write and explain the concept their group has developed for building their model bridge.
   Choice 2
      Using the Six Steps of Inventing, have the students each write to explain the way they worked as an inventor through the fourth step.

 Collaborative Teacher Activity

Building Bridges

I.   Materials: paper, pencils, graphic organizer for the Six Steps of Inventing, glue (either craft glue or a cool glue gun), box of toothpicks per group or package of Popsicle sticks per group (from craft store)
II.   Instructions
   1. Tell the students they will be building their bridges today. They will begin by using their sketches made from the library lesson.
   2. They'll also be testing their model bridges to see how strong they are.
III.   Activity
   1. Review the two kinds of structural supports they will use—arches or trusses.
   2. Read the directions on page 29 of the book.
   3. Practice making the tic-tac-toe design for the arch bridge groups.
   4. Allow time for the students to construct their bridges.

5. Test the strength of the model bridges with items from around the classroom. Have them try a pencil, a pair of scissors, tape, a stapler, etc.

6. Lead a discussion about which bridge design seemed to be stronger and why.

IV. Reflect

1. Have the groups talk about what they learned about design by doing the bridge activity.

2. Each student will take a turn in the group and tell something they noticed or how it could be improved.

V. Assessment

Choice 1

Have the students write to explain the process they used to build their bridge. Relate their process to the steps an inventor takes.

Choice 2

Write an explanation about how an arch works or a truss works.

Extension Activities

1. Have the students do an interactive bridge building activity from PBS (http://www.pbs.org/wgbh/buildingbig/bridge/challenge/index.html).

2. Build a second bridge using the same support system and this time improve on the design. Test it to see if the bridge can support more weight than the original bridge did.

3. Research and read about a famous bridge. Identify the support system it used. Report on the bridge by either writing about it or reporting back to the class.

4. Investigate a cantilever bridge support and compare it with the BATS supports.

5. After reading the book, have the students write a short description of the main idea of the book. Use the phrase, "I am an engineer. I know that _____."

Modifications for Grades K–2

1. Discuss the meaning of a bridge.
2. Show the students examples of the different kinds of bridge supports.

Language Standards (5)

Conventions of Standard English

1. Demonstrate command of the conventions of standard English grammar and usage when writing or speaking.

2. Demonstrate command of the conventions of standard English capitalization, punctuation, and spelling when writing.

Knowledge of Language

3. Apply knowledge of language to understand how language functions in different contexts, to make effective choices for meaning or style, and to comprehend more fully when reading or listening.

Vocabulary Acquisition and Use

4. Determine or clarify the meaning of unknown and multiple-meaning words and phrases by using context clues, analyzing meaningful word parts, and consulting general and specialized reference materials, as appropriate.

6. Acquire and use accurately a range of general academic and domain-specific words and phrases sufficient for reading, writing, speaking, and listening at the college and career readiness level; demonstrate independence in gathering vocabulary

knowledge when encountering an unknown term important to comprehension or expression.

Mathematical Practices (8)

1. Make sense of problems and persevere in solving them.

2. Reason abstractly and quantitatively.

3. Construct viable arguments and critique the reasoning of others.

4. Model with mathematics.

5. Use appropriate tools strategically.

6. Attend to precision.

7. Look for and make use of structure.

8. Look for and express regularity in repeated reasoning.

Mathematical Content (14)

Operations and Algebraic Thinking
* Use the four operations with whole numbers to solve problems.
* Generate and analyze patterns.

Number and Operations in Base Ten
* Use place value understanding and properties of operations to per-

3. Explain the job of a bridge engineer.
4. Use the graphic organizer to let them draw an example of each kind of support.
5. Have each student make a toothpick tic-tac-toe frame.
6. Put together a class bridge using their individual forms.
7. Have the students write about the process of making a bridge.

Differentiation strategies:

1. Discuss, define, or review pertinent vocabulary and scientific principles of the assignment after reading the book.
2. Use strategic grouping for the activity.
3. Have the students work to design and make their own bridge individually.
4. Extend the assignment to include an explanation of the four kinds of bridge supports.
5. Allow the students to decide on and present their information in any way they choose.
6. Build a class bridge to reduce the amount of time needed to construct one.
7. Ask the groups to write their information on one graphic organizer for the entire group to use.
8. Show the students the four kinds of bridge supports before they begin the lesson.
9. Prepare a set of images that show more than one example of the different kinds of bridges.

Resources:

Information about bridges and supports
http://www.pbs.org/wgbh/buildingbig/bridge/basics.html

More detailed information about bridge supports and the forces acting on them
http://science.howstuffworks.com/engineering/civil/bridge1.htm

More details on how to build a truss bridge of Popsicle sticks
http://www.instructables.com/id/Popsicle-Stick-Bridge/

Interactive bridge-building activity
http://www.pbs.org/wgbh/buildingbig/bridge/
    challenge/index.html

Build a suspension bridge
http://www.pbs.org/wgbh/buildingbig/educator/
    act_suspension_ei.html

Read about people who build bridges
http://www.pbs.org/wgbh/buildingbig/profile/index
    .html

Video about bridge building
http://www.sciencekids.co.nz/videos/engineering/
    bridgebuilding.html

Exemplar Texts:

*Bridges and Tunnels: Investigate Feats of Engineering with
    25 Projects.*
By Donna Latham. Nomad, 2012. 128p. (9781936749515)
Grade Level: 4–6
Lexile Level: IG 870L
Dewey: 624.2

*Earth-Friendly Buildings, Bridges and More: The Eco-Journal
    of Corry LaPont.*
By Etta Kaner. Kids Can Press, 2012. 64p.
    (9781554535705)
Grade Level: 3–6
ATOS Reading Level: 6.1
Lexile Level: 910L
Dewey: 720.47

Graphing Buildings and Structures.
By Yvonne Thorpe. Heinemann, 2009. 32p.
    (9780618448876)
Grade Level: 3–5
ATOS Reading Level: 4.7
Lexile Level: IG 960L
Dewey: 001.4

The Brooklyn Bridge.
By Lynn Curlee. Atheneum, 2001. 40p. (9780689831836)
Grade Level: 3–6
ATOS Reading Level: 8.2

form multi-digit
arithmetic.

**Number and
Operations—Fractions**
- Use equivalent fractions
  as a strategy to add and
  subtract fractions.
- Apply and extend
  previous understand-
  ings of multiplication
  and division to multi-
  ply and divide
  fractions.
- Develop understanding
  of fractions as numbers.

Measurement and Data
- Solve problems involv-
  ing measurement and
  estimation of intervals
  of time, liquid volumes,
  and masses of objects.
- Convert like measure-
  ment units within a
  given measurement
  system.
- Represent and interpret
  data.
- Geometric measure-
  ment: understand
  concepts of area and
  relate area to multiplication and to addition.
- Geometric measure-
  ment: recognize perim-
  eter as an attribute of
  plane figures and
  distinguish between
  linear and area
  measures.

Geometry
- Reason with shapes and
  their attributes.
- Draw and identify lines
  and angles, and classify
  shapes by properties of
  their lines and angles.

- Graph points on the coordinate plane to solve real-world and mathematical problems.

Lexile Level: 1160L
Dewey: 624

Twenty-One Elephants and Still Standing: A Story of P.T. Barnum and the Brooklyn Bridge.
By April Jones Prince. Houghton Mifflin, 2005. 32p. (9780618448876)
Grade Level: 1–5
ATOS Reading Level: 4.3
Lexile Level: AD 800L
Dewey: E

17

Cool Engineering Activities for Girls

By Heather E. Schwartz. Capstone Press, 2012. 32p. (9781429676779)

Grade Level: 3–5 *(Grades K–2 with modifications)*
Guided Reading Level: S
Lexile Level: IG 740L (Illustrated Guide)
Dewey: 607
Subject Area: engineering, science, writing

Essential Question: How can engineering help me solve problems?

Unit Summary: Students will examine the essential question, "How can engineering help me solve problems?" Students will solve an actual engineering problem by designing and testing a paper airplane. They will test their products and have the opportunity to work in groups to redesign a second plane after examining the more successful plane designs. They will use the steps an engineer might follow to address the problem and design a solution, and then retest it.

Vocabulary: accelerates, bonded, circuit, contaminants, creatively, current, engineering, friction, innovations, latex, materials, molecules, pigments, properties, recyclable, results, solar, solutions, stabilize, thermal energy, vibration

Approximate lesson time: two to three class periods

Common Core State Standards (49 total)

Reading Standards (4)

Key Ideas and Details

1. Read closely to determine what the text says explicitly and to make logical inferences from it; cite specific textual evidence when writing or speaking to support conclusions drawn from the text.

2. Determine central ideas or themes of a text and analyze their development; summarize the key supporting details and ideas.

Integration of Knowledge and Ideas

7. Integrate and evaluate content presented in diverse media and formats, including visually and quantitatively, as well as in words.

Range of Reading and Level of Text Complexity

10. Read and comprehend complex literary and informational texts independently and proficiently.

Writing Standards (9)

Text Types and Purposes

2. Write informative/ explanatory texts to examine and convey complex ideas and information clearly and accurately through the effective selection, organization, and analysis of content.

3. Write narratives to develop real or imagined experiences or events using effective technique, well-chosen details, and well-structured event sequences.

Production and Distribution of Writing

4. Produce clear and coherent writing in which the development, organization, and style are appropriate to task, purpose, and audience.

5. Develop and strengthen writing as needed by planning, revising, editing, rewriting, or trying a new approach.

6. Use technology, including the Internet, to produce and publish writing and to interact and collaborate with others.

Booktalk: Have you ever had a problem that you wanted solved? You can daydream all kinds of crazy solutions. Sometimes there aren't solutions to problems— so you have to come up with a new invention. That's what engineers do. They think creatively to solve problems and develop some fascinating innovations. How can you act like an engineer? Take a look at the book *Cool Engineering Activities for Girls*.

Book Time

1. Share the booktalk for *Cool Engineering Activities for Girls* (above). Read one of the examples from the book and lead a discussion relating it to the steps engineers use to solve problems. Then discuss the title and talk about why the students think it isn't just for girls. Talk about the pros and cons of having the word *girl* in the title.

2. In small groups or as a class, challenge the students to identify a problem they've encountered, share it, and brainstorm ways it could be solved.

✎ *Suggested lesson break.*

 Library Activity

Think Like an Engineer

I. Materials: sheets of computer paper, two or three paper clips per student, list of the steps engineers take to solve a problem in a handout or posted where the class can see (use the section in the engineering introduction), graphic organizer

II. Instructions

1. Ask the students to give their definition of engineer.

2. Define engineer and tell the students they will be working like engineers today. Refer to the definition and steps in the introductory section.

3. They will be working on their own to design and build a paper airplane that will fly well.

III. Procedure
1. Give each student a sheet of computer paper and two or three paper clips.
2. Ask each one to make a single paper airplane. They will test the airplanes after they are completed.
3. Remind them they will work as individuals, so don't discuss their design with anyone.
4. Allow time for the students to make their airplanes.
5. In small groups, have the students line up and throw their airplanes. Ask them to notice how their airplane performed.
6. Back in their seats, tell the students they will have a chance to redesign their airplanes. Give them a second sheet of paper.

Suggested lesson break.

IV. Redesign
1. Put the students in small groups. Have them take their airplanes with them as they move into their groups.
2. Have the students discuss their airplanes and what design worked best.
3. With a new sheet of paper, have the students design their own airplane in the group. Remind them to notice any changes they make in the second design. They may or may not use the same design.
4. Test this round of airplanes.
5. Instruct the students to keep their airplanes to use with the collaborating teacher.
6. Lead a discussion centered around the essential question.

V. Reflect
1. Ask the students to think about how they worked as engineers today.
2. Ask the students to identify the problem they had to solve by discussing it in their groups.
3. Give the students a small amount of time in their groups to discuss what they learned and show or explain how they changed their designs.

Research to Build and Present Knowledge

7. Conduct short as well as more sustained research projects based on focused questions, demonstrating understanding of the subject under investigation.

8. Gather relevant information from multiple print and digital sources, assess the credibility and accuracy of each source, and integrate the information while avoiding plagiarism.

9. Draw evidence from literary or informational texts to support analysis, reflection, and research.

Range of Writing

10. Write routinely over extended time frames (time for research, reflection, and revision) and shorter time frames (a single sitting or a day or two) for a range of tasks, purposes, and audiences.

Speaking and Listening Standards (5)

Comprehension and Collaboration

1. Prepare for and participate effectively in a range of conversations and collaborations with diverse partners, building on others' ideas and expressing their own clearly and persuasively.

2. Integrate and evaluate information presented in diverse media and formats, including visually, quantitatively, and orally.

Presentation of Knowledge and Ideas

4. Present information, findings, and supporting evidence such that listeners can follow the line of reasoning and the organization, development, and style are appropriate to task, purpose, and audience.

5. Make strategic use of digital media and visual displays of data to express information and enhance understanding of presentations.

6. Adapt speech to a variety of contexts and communicative tasks, demonstrating command of formal English when indicated or appropriate.

Language Standards (5)

Conventions of Standard English

1. Demonstrate command of the conventions of standard English grammar and usage when writing or speaking.

2. Demonstrate command of the conventions of standard English capitalization, punctuation, and spelling when writing.

VI. Assessment
Choice 1
Ask the students to write a paragraph explaining how they acted as engineers with their airplane activity.
Choice 2
Using the list of steps engineers follow, have the students write an example of how they incorporated each step in their airplane development and improvement.

Collaborative Teacher Activity

Let It Fly!

I. Materials: airplanes from library activity, yardsticks and meter sticks, paper to record measurements

II. Instructions
1. Using the airplanes from the library activity, toss and then measure the distance each plane flies. Do this activity in small groups to reduce the time spent watching.
2. Record the results for each airplane on a group chart in meters and centimeters and yards and inches.

III. Activity
1. Test the airplanes from the library activity in groups. Measure the distances in standard and metric units for the plane of each student in that group.
2. Record the data on the graphic organizer.
3. Using graph paper, have the students construct a bar graph to show the distances for each airplane in their group using both measuring systems.
4. Have the students with the longest distance from each group talk about the attributes that made his/her plane work so well.
5. Discuss what problems they encountered and how they addressed it in the second plane.

IV. Assessment
Write an explanation of the successes and failures of your airplane. Explain what design changes you saw work and what could be im-

proved upon to make the next airplane better or fly farther.

Extension Activities

1. Have the students identify a problem they have in their daily life and design an invention that would help solve that problem.
2. Identify the science behind one or more of the engineering activities from the book and list the terms where everyone can see them. Then have students or groups look up the terms and report back to the class by groups or individually. This is an opportunity to include technology in their search for the science vocabulary.
3. Choose an activity from the book and read it to the group. Then have the students identify the problem, who needs it, and why by writing their answers. In small groups, have them discuss their answers.
4. Have each student make a new airplane and test them individually. Measure how far they fly and see if they have improved on their designs following the lesson.
5. After reading the book, have the students write a short description of the main idea of the book. Use the phrase, "I am an engineer. I know that _____."

Modifications for Grades K–2

1. Explain the job of an engineer using the definition in the introductory section.
2. Show the class ways of making a paper airplane using the animated site.
3. Then have the students make their own planes individually.
4. Test them, and in groups have them explain why they think theirs worked or didn't work as well.
5. Provide a second sheet of paper and ask them to redesign their plane and discuss ways to improve it as they work.
6. Retest the planes.
7. Then tell them the steps an engineer takes to design a solution to the problem.
8. As a class, discuss an example of each step used in their airplane design.

Knowledge of Language

3. Apply knowledge of language to understand how language functions in different contexts, to make effective choices for meaning or style, and to comprehend more fully when reading or listening.

Vocabulary Acquisition and Use

4. Determine or clarify the meaning of unknown and multiple-meaning words and phrases by using context clues, analyzing meaningful word parts, and consulting general and specialized reference materials, as appropriate.

6. Acquire and use accurately a range of general academic and domain-specific words and phrases sufficient for reading, writing, speaking, and listening at the college and career readiness level; demonstrate independence in gathering vocabulary knowledge when encountering an unknown term important to comprehension or expression.

Mathematical Practices (8)

1. Make sense of problems and persevere in solving them.

2. Reason abstractly and quantitatively.

3. Construct viable arguments and critique the reasoning of others.

4. Model with mathematics.

5. Use appropriate tools strategically.

6. Attend to precision.

7. Look for and make use of structure.

8. Look for and express regularity in repeated reasoning.

Mathematical Content (18)

Operations and Algebraic Thinking
- Analyze patterns and relationships.

Number and Operations in Base Ten
- Use place value understanding and properties of operations to perform multi-digit arithmetic.
- Perform operations with multi-digit whole numbers and with decimals to hundredths.

Number and Operations—Fractions
- Develop understanding of fractions as numbers.
- Use equivalent fractions as a strategy to add and subtract fractions.

Measurement and Data
- Measure lengths indirectly and by iterating length units.

Differentiation strategies:

1. Discuss, define, or review pertinent vocabulary and scientific principles of the assignment after reading the book.
2. Use strategic grouping for the activity.
3. Model how to make paper airplanes before beginning the library activity.
4. Explain and discuss the steps an engineer takes before beginning the activity.
5. Use the steps as a model and take each step when making the airplane together as a group.
6. Have the students make more than two airplanes.
7. Adjust the assignments to reflect the age groups with whom you are using the lesson.
8. Have the students measure using both standard units and metric or only one.
9. Prepare a graphing page ahead of time and label the units and places for the names along the side.

Resources:

How to make a paper airplane
http://www.10paperairplanes.com/

Making a paper airplane
http://www.exploratorium.edu/exploring/paper/airplanes.html

The science behind paper airplanes
http://www.eecs.berkeley.edu/Programs/doublex/spring02/paperairplane.html

General information and the process
http://srel.uga.edu/kidsdoscience/kidsdoscience-airplanes.htm

Exemplar Texts:

How Do Jets Work?
By Buffy Silverman. Lerner, 2013. 32p. (9780761389675)
Grade Level: K–2
ATOS Reading Level: 2.9
Dewey: 629.132

Night Flight: Amelia Earhart Crosses the Atlantic.
By Robert Burleigh. Simon & Schuster, 2011. 40p.
 (9781416967330)
Grade Level: 1–4
ATOS Reading Level: 3.5
Lexile Level: AD 500L
Dewey: 629.1309163

The Hallelujah Flight.
By Phil Bildner. Putnam, 2010. 32p. (9780399247897)
Grade Level: K–3
ATOS Reading Level: 3.9
Lexile Level: AD 760L
Dewey: E

The Kids' Guide to Paper Airplanes.
By Christopher L. Harbo. Capstone, 2009. 32p.
 (9781429622745)
Grade Level: 4–7
Lexile Level: IG 640L
Dewey: 745.592

Why Do Airplanes Fly?: All About Flight.
By Rob Moore. Rosen, 2010. 24p. (9781615318902)
Grade Level: 4–6
ATOS Reading Level: 6.3
Dewey: 629.132

- Measure and estimate lengths in standard units.
- Solve problems involving measurement and estimation of intervals of time, liquid volumes, and masses of objects.
- Solve problems involving measurement and conversion of measurements from a larger unit to a smaller unit.
- Convert like measurement units within a given measurement system.
- Represent and interpret data.
- Geometric measurement: understand concepts of angle and measure angles.
- Geometric measurement: understand concepts of volume and relate volume to multiplication and to addition.

Geometry
- Identify and describe shapes.
- Analyze, compare, create, and compose shapes.
- Reason with shapes and their attributes.
- Draw and identify lines and angles, and classify shapes by properties of their lines and angles.
- Graph points on the coordinate plane to solve real-world and mathematical problems.

18

Cranes

By Amanda Doering Tourville.
ABDO, 2009. 32p. (9781602706224)

Grade Level: 3–5 *(Grades K–2 with modifications)*
ATOS Reading Level: 4.0
Guided Reading Level: P
Dewey: 621.8
Subject Area: engineering, science, reading, writing

Essential Question: "How do simple machines help cranes work?"

Unit Summary: Students will examine the essential question, "How do simple machines help cranes work?" Working in small groups, students will research the basic simple machines: inclined plane, wedge, screw, lever, pulley, wheel, and axle. They will organize their research into four categories and present and post it in the room so other students can find out about the other simple machines used in cranes. They will use their graphic organizer to write and explain about the value of cranes, the kinds, and what makes them work.

Vocabulary: boom, cables, counterweights, force, hook, inclined plane, jib, lever, load, outriggers, pulleys, screw, wedge, wheel and axle

Approximate lesson time: one to two class periods

Booktalk: When a brand new skyscraper goes up, how do the construction workers get the very heavy materials needed up to the top of a tall, tall building? They use a crane. There are a variety of different kinds of cranes to use for different kinds of jobs. There's even one special

Common Core State Standards (38 total)

Reading Standards (7)

Key Ideas and Details

1. Read closely to determine what the text says explicitly and to make logical inferences from it; cite specific textual evidence when writing or speaking to support conclusions drawn from the text.

2. Determine central ideas or themes of a text and analyze their development; summarize the key supporting details and ideas.

3. Analyze how and why individuals, events, and ideas develop and interact over the course of a text.

Craft and Structure

4. Interpret words and phrases as they are used in a text, including determining technical, connotative,

and figurative meanings, and analyze how specific word choices shape meaning or tone.

Integration of Knowledge and Ideas

7. Integrate and evaluate content presented in diverse media and formats, including visually and quantitatively, as well as in words.

8. Delineate and evaluate the argument and specific claims in a text, including the validity of the reasoning as well as the relevance and sufficiency of the evidence.

Range of Reading and Level of Text Complexity

10. Read and comprehend complex literary and informational texts independently and proficiently.

Writing Standards (8)

Text Types and Purposes

1. Write arguments to support claims in an analysis of substantive topics or texts, using valid reasoning and relevant and sufficient evidence.

2. Write informative/explanatory texts to examine and convey complex ideas and information clearly and accurately through the effective selection, organization, and analysis of content.

crane at Sea World to lift killer whales out of their tanks. Other cranes are used to lift heavy loads and move up tall skyscrapers as the building goes up. There are four main types of cranes. What are they? Take a look at the book *Cranes*.

Book Time

1. Share the booktalk for *Cranes* (above).
2. Read the book through to the end.

✎ *Suggested lesson break.*

 Library Activity

Simple Machines at Work

I. Materials: notebook paper, pencils, reference books, computers, books about simple machines, a note-taking page listing the six simple machines, and a place for writing facts and a glossary

II. Instructions
1. Tell the students that they will be finding out information about simple machines and where they are located in a crane.
2. They will be looking up their simple machine, then making a diagram and writing a definition for it. The cranes they learned about in the book are a combination of simple machines. That makes it a compound machine. Tell them they will focus today on simple machines.
3. Put the students into six groups. Assign each group one simple machine to research: inclined plane, wedge, screw, lever, pulley, wheel, and axle

III. Procedure
1. Tell the students they will work in their groups.
2. Define the words *effort* and *load* as used in engineering and science. Effort: the force applied to an object; load: the resistance or weight you are trying to move. Point out how the two words show opposing forces and are opposites.

✎ *Suggested lesson break.*

3. Tell the groups that they will create and present a poster showing four things: a diagram of their simple machine with labels, an example of their simple machine, a written definition of their machine including how it makes work easier, and two vocabulary words with pronunciation and definitions that would fit into a glossary. Add that in one of the squares, they must include where their simple machine is found on one of the kinds of cranes. Use the graphic organizer to review these points.

4. Emphasize the fact that they will use the glossary, index, table of contents from their books, and links to help them find their information. Review the locations of the glossary, index, and table of contents, and review their uses and show them in a book. Review links on the computer.

5. Allow enough time for the groups to research and design their posters.

Suggested lesson break.

6. Have each group present their posters.

7. Put the posters around the room. Have the students move from poster to poster and fill in two facts on their graphic organizer. Then they will write down the two vocabulary words.

8. Review the six simple machines using the student posters to close the lesson and then discuss the essential question and answer it.

V. Reflect

1. Have the students pair/share about their machine. Ask each one to tell the other person one thing about each of the six simple machines using their vocabulary notes.

2. Have them refer to their note page if they don't remember and repeat the pair/share.

3. Notice where simple machines are found in cranes.

VI. Assessment

Choice 1

Use the student posters and presentations to assess their work done on the posters.

Production and Distribution of Writing

4. Produce clear and coherent writing in which the development, organization, and style are appropriate to task, purpose, and audience.

5. Develop and strengthen writing as needed by planning, revising, editing, rewriting, or trying a new approach.

Research to Build and Present Knowledge

7. Conduct short as well as more sustained research projects based on focused questions, demonstrating understanding of the subject under investigation.

8. Gather relevant information from multiple print and digital sources, assess the credibility and accuracy of each source, and integrate the information while avoiding plagiarism.

9. Draw evidence from literary or informational texts to support analysis, reflection, and research.

Range of Writing

10. Write routinely over extended time frames (time for research, reflection, and revision) and shorter time frames (a single sitting or a day or two) for a range of tasks, purposes, and audiences.

Choice 2

Have the students write about their simple machine and use two of the vocabulary words they found.

⚙ Collaborative Teacher Activity

Cranes at Work

I. Materials: notebook paper, pencils, page listing selected vocabulary words about crane parts (See following vocabulary list.) You will also need two graphic organizers. One is in the appendix and the other is online (http://www.eduplace.com/graphicorganizer/pdf/cluster.pdf).

The following vocabulary list shows the parts of a crane.

   a. jib—a piece on the crane's arm that makes the boom longer
   b. hook—a strong, curved piece of metal hanging from the steel cables that lift the load
   c. cables—thick, strong, rope-like strands of metal to hold weight
   d. boom—the long steel arm of a crane
   e. pulleys—a simple machine that decreases effort when lifting a load
   f. outriggers—strong metal pieces at the bottom of a rough terrain crane to hold it steady
   g. counterweights—weights at the back of the crane to balance the load so it doesn't tip forward

II. Instructions

   1. Tell the students that together they will identify the main idea of the book and post it as a phrase where everyone can see it. Have the students practice stating the main idea of the book in a complete sentence. When several students have commented, come to a group consensus about the main idea and write it down.
   2. Together, identify the four main kinds of cranes and write those names near the main idea.

3. Tell the students that today they will use a graphic organizer to show the main idea of the book and identify the important facts about cranes.

4. They will add the names of the four kinds of cranes and add details about each of them.

5. Then they will write about cranes and explain why they are useful.

6. Review the vocabulary words.

III. Procedure

1. Tell the students they will work individually.

2. Have the students make a graphic organizer or use the link to make a preprinted organizer using a central oval, four ovals extending from that, and two or three ovals from each of the four.

3. In the center oval, have the students write the word "crane." Then have them include the main idea of the book below it and written as a sentence.

4. Reread pages 10–15 and review the four kinds of cranes. Show the book to the class and project it so everyone can see the spread. Fill in the four ovals extending from the center oval with the word crane in it.

5. Return to page 10 and read the text boxes. Have the students add the information to the first oval (tower crane) on the graphic organizer. Tell them they might not fill all the boxes. You may need to help with the wording. Continue with pages 11–15 and have the students fill in their ovals for each kind of crane.

6. Add ovals to the graphic organizer as you read the remainder of the book, stopping to point out information. Remind them to notice and write why cranes are important.

7. Return to the introduction and read it, and then read the closing. Point out how the book begins and concludes.

8. Have the students write to explain the uses, kinds, and importance of cranes using their graphic organizers to help them. Remind them to support their main ideas with facts, definitions, and details and to use connecting words.

Language Standards (6)

Conventions of Standard English

1. Demonstrate command of the conventions of standard English grammar and usage when writing or speaking.

2. Demonstrate command of the conventions of standard English capitalization, punctuation, and spelling when writing.

Knowledge of Language

3. Apply knowledge of language to understand how language functions in different contexts, to make effective choices for meaning or style, and to comprehend more fully when reading or listening.

Vocabulary Acquisition and Use

4. Determine or clarify the meaning of unknown and multiple-meaning words and phrases by using context clues, analyzing meaningful word parts, and consulting general and specialized reference materials, as appropriate.

5. Demonstrate understanding of figurative language, word relationships, and nuances in word meanings.

6. Acquire and use accurately a range of general academic and domain-specific words and phrases

sufficient for reading, writing, speaking, and listening at the college and career readiness level; demonstrate independence in gathering vocabulary knowledge when encountering an unknown term important to comprehension or expression.

Mathematical Practices (8)

1. Make sense of problems and persevere in solving them.

2. Reason abstractly and quantitatively.

3. Construct viable arguments and critique the reasoning of others.

5. Use appropriate tools strategically.

6. Attend to precision.

7. Look for and make use of structure.

8. Look for and express regularity in repeated reasoning.

Mathematical Content (4)

Operations and Algebraic Thinking

• Analyze patterns and relationships.

Measurement and Data

• Solve problems involving measurement and estimation of intervals

9. Allow enough time for the students to complete their writing.
10. Have volunteers read their written summaries.

V. Reflect
1. Have the students read their writing silently to check and see if they have explained what they intended to and to see if their details supported their ideas.
2. Have the students exchange papers and read them to one another in pairs. Tell them to discuss and ask questions about parts they don't understand or parts they think could have been expressed more clearly.

VI. Assessment
Choice 1
Use the student papers to assess their work.
Choice 2
Have the students write about how the graphic organizer helped them organize their ideas and talk about one of the cranes from the book that most interested them.

Extension Activities

1. Group the students and have them draw a diagram of one of the kinds of cranes and label it.
2. Read another book about cranes and together compare and contrast the ideas presented in the two books.
3. Use the information from the library activity and create a class glossary by combining and alphabetizing the words.
4. Look up the bird called a crane. Find out about the different varieties of cranes and report to the group. Explain why the machine is called a crane.
5. After reading the book, have the students write a short description of the main idea of the book. Use the phrase, "I am an engineer. I know that _____."

Modifications for Grades K–2

1. Pre-select books about simple machines and have the students look up one of the main six kinds of simple machines in small groups.
2. Have them read about their assigned machine. One of the facts they need to find is how their machine makes work easier.
3. Use the graphic organizer to help them organize the information they find.
4. Students can present their information to the class or put it on a poster.
5. Have them list the different kinds of simple machines and write down one thing they learned about each one from the other groups.
6. As a large group, look at a diagram of the cranes and identify some of the simple machines.

> of time, liquid volumes, and masses of objects.
> • Represent and interpret data.
>
> **Geometry**
> • Reason with shapes and their attributes.

Differentiation strategies:

1. Discuss, define, or review pertinent vocabulary and scientific principles of the assignment before or after reading the book.
2. Use strategic grouping for the activity.
3. Use the graphic organizer to guide their work or have them create their own organizer after researching on their own.
4. Have the students work individually rather than in groups.
5. Allow the students to determine their method of conveying their information.
6. Have the students incorporate technology into their presentations.
7. Extend the length of the assignment to cover more information in the final products.
8. Prepare a set of images of simple machines and review them before beginning the lesson.
9. Use images of cranes either before or after the lesson to show the kinds of simple machines incorporated in them.
10. Ask the groups to write their information on only one graphic organizer for the entire group.

Resources:

Graphic organizer for collaborative activity
http://www.eduplace.com/graphicorganizer/pdf/cluster.pdf

Source for simple machine explanations
http://www.uark.edu/depts/aeedhp/agscience/simpmach.htm

How to build a model crane with Legos
http://www.eng.iastate.edu/twt/Courses/Undergrad/packet/machine%20directions/pulleys2.htm

Links in the first paragraph to the different kinds of cranes with an explanation.
http://www.naicranes.com/?gclid=CO
   _BuMeijLYCFWGrPAodyBoAYw

Definitions with pictures
http://www.edheads.org/activities/simple-machines/glossary.shtml

Exemplar Texts:

Explore Simple Machines! 25 Great Projects, Activities, Experiments.
By Anita Yasuda. Nomad, 2011. 96p. (9781936313822)
Grade Level: 2–4
Lexile Level: 830L
Dewey: 621.8

Move It!   Work It!: A Song about Simple Machines.
By Laura Purdie Salas. Picture Window Books, 2009. 24p. (9781404852990)
Grade Level: 1–3
Lexile Level: 710L
Dewey: 621

Simple Machines.
By Ade Deane-Pratt. PowerKids Press, 2012. 32p. (9781448852796)
Grade Level: 3–5
ATOS Reading Level: 5.2
Dewey: 621.8

Simple Machines.
By JoAnn Early Macken. Amicus, 2011. 24p. (9781607530169)
Grade Level: PreK–2
ATOS Reading Level: 1.8
Dewey: 621.8

Simple Machines.
By Dana Meachen Rau. Children's Press, 2012. 48p. (9780531263242)
Grade Level: 3–5
ATOS Reading Level: 4.9
Lexile Level: 780L
Dewey: 621.8

19

Pop! The Invention of Bubble Gum

By Meghan McCarthy. Simon & Schuster, 2010. 32p. (9781416979708)

Grade Level: 3–5 *(Grades K–2 with modifications)*
ATOS Reading Level: 4.8
Lexile Level: AD 740L (Adult Directed)
Dewey: 664.6
Subject Area: engineering, science, writing

Essential Question: "How was the invention of bubble gum engineered?"

Unit Summary: Students will examine the essential question, "How was the invention of bubble gum engineered?" They will review the steps engineers take when they explore a solution to a problem. They will then determine the steps Walter Diemer took to create bubble gum after listening to the text of the book and apply and explain his ideas and actions the way an engineer works to solve a problem. They will present their information and discuss their finding in a large group.

Vocabulary: accountant, batch, beakers, budgets, experimental, factory, flavoring, ingredients, invention, laboratory, mastic tree, sap, stomachaches

Approximate lesson time: one to two class periods

Booktalk: Have you ever wondered about where bubble gum came from? Gum has been around for a long

Common Core State Standards (45 total)

Reading Standards (6)

Key Ideas and Details

1. Read closely to determine what the text says explicitly and to make logical inferences from it; cite specific textual evidence when writing or speaking to support conclusions drawn from the text.

2. Determine central ideas or themes of a text and analyze their development; summarize the key supporting details and ideas.

3. Analyze how and why individuals, events, and ideas develop and interact over the course of a text.

Integration of Knowledge and Ideas

7. Integrate and evaluate content presented in diverse media and formats, including visually and quantitatively, as well as in words.

8. Delineate and evaluate the argument and specific claims in a text, including the validity of the reasoning as well as the relevance and sufficiency of the evidence.

Range of Reading and Level of Text Complexity

10. Read and comprehend complex literary and informational texts independently and proficiently.

Writing Standards (9)

Text Types and Purposes

1. Write arguments to support claims in an analysis of substantive topics or texts, using valid reasoning and relevant and sufficient evidence.

3. Write narratives to develop real or imagined experiences or events using effective technique, well-chosen details, and well-structured event sequences.

Production and Distribution of Writing

4. Produce clear and coherent writing in which the development, organization, and style are

time. But bubble gum has not! Somebody had to think of the idea of adding flavors and colors—and how to blow bubbles, too. So who made bubble gum and how long ago did they invent it? Let's read about the man who invented bubble gum and examine the problems and persistence he used to solve his problem. Take a look at the book *Pop! The Invention of Bubble Gum.*

Book Time

1. Share the booktalk for *Pop! The Invention of Bubble Gum* (above). Read the book to the students.
2. Ask the students how Walter Diemer acted as an engineer. Review the steps an engineer takes to solve a problem with the class.

Suggested lesson break.

Library Activity

The Bubble Gum Engineer

I. Materials: paper, list of the steps engineers take to solve a problem (in a size the class can see or a printed copy) taken from the introductory notes about engineering, graphic organizer

II. Instructions

1. Tell the students that today they will show the ways in which Walter Diemer worked as an engineer.
2. In small groups, have the students review the list of steps engineers take to solve a problem, and then apply them to the steps Walter took to solve his problem. You may want to print out the steps engineers take to investigate or solve a problem or display them so everyone can see them.

III. Procedure

1. Group the students into four or five per group.
2. Tell them you'll reread the book. As you do, they will take notes for their activity about how the steps Walter took while engineering his bubble gum. You might want to let

them take their notes directly onto the graphic organizer.

3. Reread the book.

4. Give the students time to work together to name Walter's steps and write them down. Have each student write his/her own copy, even though they are discussing it in a group.

5. Decide how you want the students to present their information and then lead a discussion about how Walter Diemer acted as an engineer to answer the essential question.

V. Reflect

1. Let the groups discuss their ideas following the large group discussion or presentations they made.

2. Allow time for the students to make any changes they wish to their papers.

VI. Assessment

Choice 1

Have the students individually write and explain Walter's steps to producing bubble gum and relate them the way he worked as an engineer.

Choice 2

Have the students write an explanation of the process Walter used to develop bubble gum and support it both with details from the book and the steps engineers use to problem solve.

Collaborative Teacher Activity

Chew, Chew!

I. Materials: graph paper, two different brands of bubble gum (one of both for every student and as near to the same size as possible), a stopwatch (or stopwatch app)

II. Instructions

1. Tell the students they will be making qualitative and quantitative observations about their gum today.

2. They'll also be testing their gum to measure how long the sugar lasts (that is what gives the gum most of its flavor) and comparing the two different brands. Tell them they will be

appropriate to task, purpose, and audience.

5. Develop and strengthen writing as needed by planning, revising, editing, rewriting, or trying a new approach.

6. Use technology, including the Internet, to produce and publish writing and to interact and collaborate with others.

Research to Build and Present Knowledge

7. Conduct short as well as more sustained research projects based on focused questions, demonstrating understanding of the subject under investigation.

8 Gather relevant information from multiple print and digital sources, assess the credibility and accuracy of each source, and integrate the information while avoiding plagiarism.

9. Draw evidence from literary or informational texts to support analysis, reflection, and research.

Range of Writing

10. Write routinely over extended time frames (time for research, reflection, and revision) and shorter time frames (a single sitting or a day or two) for a range of tasks, purposes, and audiences.

Speaking and Listening Standards (5)

Comprehension and Collaboration

1. Prepare for and participate effectively in a range of conversations and collaborations with diverse partners, building on others' ideas and expressing their own clearly and persuasively.

2. Integrate and evaluate information presented in diverse media and formats, including visually, quantitatively, and orally.

Presentation of Knowledge and Ideas

4. Present information, findings, and supporting evidence such that listeners can follow the line of reasoning and the organization, development, and style are appropriate to task, purpose, and audience.

5. Make strategic use of digital media and visual displays of data to express information and enhance understanding of presentations.

6. Adapt speech to a variety of contexts and communicative tasks, demonstrating command of formal English when indicated or appropriate.

looking for ways this test might not be a completely accurate way to test gum. Ask them to locate the ways this test might have fallacies and think about how they could improve it.

III. Activity

1. Have the students use a sheet of paper and make two columns labeled with the name of the gum. Subdivide each column into two more sections and label them qualitative and quantitative. You might want to have them turn the paper so it's in landscape direction.

2. Review the terms. Qualitative observations are those made by using the senses and quantitative observations involve measurement and numbers. *A trick to remember the difference: the N in quaNtitative = numbers.*

3. Pass out rulers and ask them to measure the gum to the nearest eighth inch. Then measure it in millimeters and centimeters and record those measurements on their paper under the quantitative section.

4. For the qualitative part, tell them as scientists they may taste the gum today by licking it, since it is a known substance and you can reassure them it's safe. Then remind them never to taste any unknown substance. Tell them not to chew it yet and keep the lick to one small taste.

5. Allow enough time for the students to record their observations. Tell them to make a time section under each gum brand.

6. Next, explain that they will be timing how long the flavor in their gum lasts using minutes and seconds. Then they'll convert the time to all seconds. Explain that most of gum's flavor comes from the sugar in it. They will chew the gum until they think they do not taste any more flavor. Tell them to be absolutely sure there is no more flavor. When they do, have them raise their hand and you'll call out their time in min-

utes and seconds. Have them record the time and convert the time to total seconds.

7. When everyone has chewed the flavor out and has a time written down, begin the second round with the next brand of bubble gum. Repeat the sequence.

8. Last, tell everyone to blow the biggest bubble possible out of the last piece of gum they chewed on the time activity. Set the completed bubble down on a paper towel. Measure the gum by marking on the paper towel from each side to estimate the diameter. Record that on their paper. You might also want them to do this with the first piece of gum when they have finished chewing it. Then compare the size of the two bubbles.

🖉 *Suggested lesson break.*

9. Divide the students into groups of four or five. Using the graph paper, have them make a bar graph to show the times in seconds that each brand of gum's flavor lasted for every person and both gums in their group. Each student should make a graph.

10. Allow enough time to complete their activity.

IV. Reflect

1. Ask one member from each group to present their information. Have the students notice if any of the data seem out of line or faulty in some way. The students will look over their own data and see if there are any discrepancies.

2. Discuss in the groups any data that doesn't seem to fit with that of the others in the group. Talk about what might have made the experiment not quite exact or accurate.

IV. Assessment

Have the students summarize the results from their group by writing about the results and then discuss in a paragraph the parts of the test they did that might have made their results inaccurate.

Language Standards (5)

Conventions of Standard English

1. Demonstrate command of the conventions of standard English grammar and usage when writing or speaking.

2. Demonstrate command of the conventions of standard English capitalization, punctuation, and spelling when writing.

Knowledge of Language

3. Apply knowledge of language to understand how language functions in different contexts, to make effective choices for meaning or style, and to comprehend more fully when reading or listening.

Vocabulary Acquisition and Use

4. Determine or clarify the meaning of unknown and multiple-meaning words and phrases by using context clues, analyzing meaningful word parts, and consulting general and specialized reference materials, as appropriate.

6. Acquire and use accurately a range of general academic and domain-specific words and phrases sufficient for reading, writing, speaking, and listening at the college and career readiness level; demonstrate independence in gathering vocabulary

knowledge when encountering an unknown term important to comprehension or expression.

Mathematical Practices (8)

1. Make sense of problems and persevere in solving them.

2. Reason abstractly and quantitatively.

3. Construct viable arguments and critique the reasoning of others.

4. Model with mathematics.

5. Use appropriate tools strategically.

6. Attend to precision.

7. Look for and make use of structure.

8. Look for and express regularity in repeated reasoning.

Mathematical Content (12)

Operations and Algebraic Thinking

- Write and interpret numerical expressions.
- Analyze patterns and relationships.

Number and Operations in Base Ten

- Understand the place value system.
- Perform operations with multi-digit whole

Extension Activities

1. Look up information about the history of bubble gum using the resources from the back of the book. Have the students report their findings in class presentations.
2. Have the students make a number line with markings to eighths on a sentence strip or sheet of paper. Hold a bubble gum blowing contest. Put their bubble on the number line and measure it from the part of the bubble that actually touches the paper (to get the most accurate measure). Compare and announce the winner.
3. Try testing gum made with sugar against sugarless gum sweetened with an artificial sweetener. Predict what they think will happen and test it. Write down their conclusions.
4. Determine the mean, median, and average for the class.
5. After reading the book, have the students write a short description of the main idea of the book. Use the phrase, "I am an engineer. I know that _____."

Modifications for Grades K–2

1. Review the steps an engineer uses to make sure the students understand the process.
2. After reading the book through, go back and, as a group, identify the steps Walter took.
3. Write down the steps on the graphic organizer.
4. Have each group discuss how Walter worked as an engineer and write a short two- or three-sentence explanation.
5. Have each group present their explanations.
6. For the collaborative activity, have a graph page prepared and labeled. Use seconds only, or convert the minutes into seconds for the students. Alternatively, do the gum blowing activity only. Graph those results.

Differentiation strategies:

1. Discuss, define, or review pertinent vocabulary before or after reading the book.
2. Use strategic grouping for the activity.

3. Have students work on their graphic organizer individually.
4. Allow the students to present their information in any way they choose.
5. Ask the groups to write their information on one graphic organizer for the entire group.
6. Discuss each step of Walter's process during the time you encounter it in the book and give the students the time to write it down then.

Resources:

More about gum and its invention
http://inventors.about.com/od/gstartinventions/a/
    gum.htm

More about Walter Diemer's invention
http://www.ideafinder.com/history/inventions/
    bubblegum.htm

Resources about gum and interesting facts
http://www.chewinggumfacts.com/

Dentists and gum
http://www.ada.org/1315.aspx

How to blow bubbles with gum
http://www.ehow.com/how_2046145_blow-bubble
    -gum.html

YouTube video on how to blow bubbles (has 15-second
    ad before video)
http://www.youtube.com/watch?v=u9SzUDm14ss

Exemplar Texts:

Bubbles Float, Bubbles Pop.
By Mark Weakland. Capstone, 2011. 32p. (9781429652506)
Grade Level: 1–3
ATOS Reading Level: 2.7
Lexile Level: NC 620L
Dewey: 530.4

Bubbles in the Bathroom.
By Susan Martineau. Windmill, 2012. 24p. (9781615318902)
Grade Level: 3–6
ATOS Reading Level: 3.6

numbers and with decimals to hundredths.

Number and Operations—Fractions
- Develop understanding of fractions as numbers.
- Solve problems involving measurement and conversion of measurements from a larger unit to a smaller unit.

Measurement and Data
- Tell and write time.
- Convert like measurement units within a given measurement system.
- Represent and interpret data.
- Geometric measurement: understand concepts of volume and relate volume to multiplication and to addition.

Geometry
- Reason with shapes and their attributes.
- Graph points on the coordinate plane to solve real-world and mathematical problems.

Dewey: 507.8

Does It Really Take Seven Years to Digest Swallowed Gum? And Other Questions You've Always Wanted to Ask.
By Sandy Donovan. Lerner, 2010. 40p. (9780822590859)
Grade Level: 4–6
ATOS Reading Level: 5.3
Lexile Level: IG 860L
Dewey: 610

Lester Fizz, Bubble-Gum Artist.
By Ruth Spiro. Dutton, 2008. 32p. (9780525478614)
Grade Level: 2–4
ATOS Reading Level: 3.0
Lexile Level: AD 520L
Dewey: E

The Tooth Book: A Guide to Healthy Teeth and Gums.
By Edward Miller. Holiday House, 2008. 32p. (9780823420926)
Grade Level: K–3
ATOS Reading Level: 4.5
Lexile Level: AD 930L
Dewey: 617.601

PART V

Teaching Mathematics in Your Library

Mathematics is . . .

Definition: Mathematics is the study of numbers, quantities, shapes, space, and measurements and how they relate to one another.

Background

The word mathematics comes from the Greek word meaning "disposed to learn." Pure mathematics studies the relationships of numbers in an abstract manner; applied mathematics is incorporated into other disciplines like physics and engineering. The formal teaching of mathematics was established around five thousand years ago by the Sumerians, about the same time as reading and writing developed.

For learners at the elementary age, standards include thinking math, which incorporates the nature of mathematical reasoning; and content math, which has to do with specific math topics. Thinking math includes problem solving, communication, reasoning, and connecting concepts. Content math includes estimation, numbers, geometry, spatial understanding, measurement, statistics, fractions and decimals, and patterns and relationships.

Problem solving for children teaches that there may be more than one way to solve a problem. Communication helps learners clarify what they are attempting to do as they search for a solution. Reasoning requires a learner to think about the problem and search for a logical, doable solution. Connections deal with relating math concepts to the real world.

Repeating patterns and relationships establishes the underlying foundation of things, so that the child can reasonably expect to know what comes next even if it isn't seen. Number sense refers to number knowledge but isn't simply counting. A strong concept of numbers and how they work and fit together is part of this skill. The physical world is filled with shapes and angles, and spatial understanding helps children relate to people and objects in their own world.

Measurement has to do with using the tools needed to understand size, distance, volume, and time. Fractions and decimals help them understand things as a part of a whole. Estimating provides a skill that gives numbers and sizes a meaning. Organizing and interpreting data through charts and graphs allows children to interpret information and see how these facts are related.

The discipline of math spans an interdisciplinary language and gives tools for managing the subject. Mathematics holds range, depth, complexity, and great beauty for the elegant way it all works together.

 **20**

A Very Improbable Story

By Edward Einhorn. Charlesbridge, 2008. 32p. (9781570918711)

Grade Level: 3–5 *(Grades 1–2 with modifications)*
ATOS Reading Level: 3.2
Lexile Level: AD 470L (Adult Directed)
Dewey: E
Subject Area: mathematics, writing

Essential Question: What is probability?

Unit Summary: Students will examine the essential question, "What is probability?" They will become familiar with probability by making predictions and then testing them. Each student will keep data about their predictions and look for patterns as they use a spinner to see which color the arrow will land on. They will use vocabulary related to probability and write a number sentence to show their information.

Vocabulary: cartwheel, certain, combinations, handstand, impossible, improbable, likely, mismatched, odds, probability, unlikely

Approximate lesson time: one to two class periods

Booktalk: What would you do if you woke up one morning with a cat stuck to your head? The last thing you'd probably think of is doing a math activity to get it off. But that's exactly the situation Ethan finds himself in. After trying any number of ways to beat the odds, can Ethan finally overcome the challenges created by a cat

Common Core State Standards (54 total)

Reading Standards (7)

Key Ideas and Details

1. Read closely to determine what the text says explicitly and to make logical inferences from it; cite specific textual evidence when writing or speaking to support conclusions drawn from the text.

2. Determine central ideas or themes of a text and analyze their development; summarize the key supporting details and ideas.

3. Analyze how and why individuals, events, and ideas develop and interact over the course of a text.

Craft and Structure

4. Interpret words and phrases as they are used in

a text, including determining technical, connotative, and figurative meanings, and analyze how specific word choices shape meaning or tone.

Integration of Knowledge and Ideas

7. Integrate and evaluate content presented in diverse media and formats, including visually and quantitatively, as well as in words.

8. Delineate and evaluate the argument and specific claims in a text, including the validity of the reasoning as well as the relevance and sufficiency of the evidence.

Range of Reading and Level of Text Complexity

10. Read and comprehend complex literary and informational texts independently and proficiently.

Writing Standards (7)

Text Types and Purposes

1. Write arguments to support claims in an analysis of substantive topics or texts, using valid reasoning and relevant and sufficient evidence.

2. Write informative/ explanatory texts to examine and convey complex ideas and information clearly and accurately through the effective selection, organization, and analysis of content.

named Odds? Or did he have to go to his big soccer match wearing Odds on his head? Let's take a look at this book titled *A Very Improbable Story* and find out.

Book Time

1. Share the booktalk for *A Very Improbable Story* (above).
2. Ask the students the meaning of improbable. Guide them to arrive at a definition of the word or look the word up to find the definition.
3. Read the book straight through.
4. After reading, discuss the story line and review the meaning of probability as it's used in the book.

 ## Library Activity

Let's All Spin

I. Materials: paper and pencils, crayons or markers, scissors, 4 red paper squares, 3 blue paper squares, 2 green squares, 1 yellow square (all the same size), brads, spinners (can be made by printing on cardstock; http://www.webeans.net/hutt/educ/spinner4_bw.pdf or http://www.webeans.net/hutt/educ/colorspinner4.pdf), graphic organizer

II. Instructions
   1. Tell the students they will be practicing probability using squares of paper.
   2. Next, they will write some probability predictions.
   3. After practicing, they will predict and test the probability of a spinner landing on a certain color and write down their results.
   4. Explain that they will predict which color comes up when they spin the arrow and then they will record which color comes up for ten spins.
   5. Tell the students that they will each take ten spins and will record the information on their graphic organizer. They'll be using this data with the collaborating teacher.

III. Procedure
   1. Introduce and define these four words: impossible, unlikely, likely, certain. After dis-

cussing the meaning, have the students write the definition for each word.

2. Show the students the colored squares. Drop all the red squares into the bag. Ask them what the probability is of pulling out a red square (certain). Then ask them what the probability is of pulling out a blue square (none, since you haven't added any to the bag yet).

3. Add the one yellow square to the bag holding the red squares. Then ask what the probability is of pulling out the yellow square. Point out how many squares are in the bag (5). Tell them the chances are 1 in 5 that you'll choose the yellow square.

4. Remove the yellow square and add the 3 blue squares. Review the total squares in the bag (7). Then ask them which word best fits with the probability of pulling out a blue square. Tell them there is a 3 out of 7 chance of choosing a blue square.

5. Continue until you have put all the squares into the bag. Each time, ask the students what chance you'll have of pulling out a particular color square.

6. Next, model examples using statements to elicit one of the four responses to practice understanding of the four words. For example, say: The sun will not rise today; We are in (name of school); We won't do any lessons today; The cafeteria will serve juice instead of milk. The students choose which of the four vocabulary responses best states the possibility of being correct. Discuss the responses and have them explain why one response is chosen over another.

7. Have the students write their own statement that can be answered with one of the four responses. Share their statements and have the class give the response.

8. Tell them that probability is based on what is likely to happen. They will make spinners and use them to collect their probability data.

9. Pass out the spinners to groups or individuals placed in groups of about three to four students each. Give each one a brad and a

Production and Distribution of Writing

4. Produce clear and coherent writing in which the development, organization, and style are appropriate to task, purpose, and audience.

5. Develop and strengthen writing as needed by planning, revising, editing, rewriting, or trying a new approach.

Research to Build and Present Knowledge

7. Conduct short as well as more sustained research projects based on focused questions, demonstrating understanding of the subject under investigation.

9. Draw evidence from literary or informational texts to support analysis, reflection, and research.

Range of Writing

10. Write routinely over extended time frames (time for research, reflection, and revision) and shorter time frames (a single sitting or a day or two) for a range of tasks, purposes, and audiences.

Speaking and Listening Standards (5)

Comprehension and Collaboration

1. Prepare for and participate effectively in a range of conversations and

collaborations with diverse partners, building on others' ideas and expressing their own clearly and persuasively.

2. Integrate and evaluate information presented in diverse media and formats, including visually, quantitatively, and orally.

Presentation of Knowledge and Ideas

4. Present information, findings, and supporting evidence such that listeners can follow the line of reasoning and the organization, development, and style are appropriate to task, purpose, and audience.

5. Make strategic use of digital media and visual displays of data to express information and enhance understanding of presentations.

6. Adapt speech to a variety of contexts and communicative tasks, demonstrating command of formal English when indicated or appropriate.

Language Standards (6)

Conventions of Standard English

1. Demonstrate command of the conventions of standard English grammar and usage when writing or speaking.

spinner arrow. Color and cut out the materials and demonstrate how to put the spinner together.

✎ *Suggested lesson break.*

10. Use the data chart to record their information before they begin spinning.
11. The students will first predict spin #1 and write down the color they think it will land on. The first student will spin his or her spinner and record the color of spin #1. Continue to predict, spin, and record the results.
12. Take turns for each round until all group members have made 10 spins.
13. Conclude the lesson by discussing anything they noticed on their information and review the essential question.
14. Ask the students to write a number sentence using their probability predictions from their spins.

IV.   Reflect
1. Ask the students to look over their data. Have them count how many times they correctly predicted their spin color.
2. Ask them to review and write down something they noticed about their results. Then have them think about what might happen if they did the activity again. Would they get the same results?

VI.   Assessment
Choice 1
Give the students examples using the colored square combinations and ask them to write the probability of drawing a particular color of square.
Choice 2
Have the students write a sentence for each of the four words used in the lesson to demonstrate their comprehension. They will model them in a way similar to the ones they made up themselves.

⌒ **Collaborative Teacher Activity**

What Colors Did You Spin?

I. Materials: graph paper, pencils, map pencils or markers

II. Instructions
 1. Read the book to the class. As you read, ask them to notice and write down when Odds challenges Ethan in a probability match.
 2. Discuss what the students noticed about the challenges.
 3. Show the students page 19. Talk about the possible combinations that resulted from those marble combinations. Explain how the odds of 100 marbles in four colors results in a 1 in 16 chance.

III. Procedure
 1. Tell the students that they will be graphing their results from the library lesson to look for patterns of probability. Then they will write about their predictions and probability and explain any patterns or trends they noticed.
 2. Model how to set up the graph. The X-axis will show the total predictions and trial results of the students' own spins. They will count up how many for each color resulted and record that number on the graph using that color. Record the predictions and the results side by side.
 3. Label the Y-axis starting from 0 and count by 1s upward.
 4. Color in the results according to their data. Each trial should be colored according to the color they predicted and spun. If time allows, have the students graph the results of their other group members.
 5. Then write the number of times each color came up for their results as a fraction. For example, if they had red come up 4 times, they would write "Red = 4/10." Reduce the probability fraction if you've covered this concept already. Do this for all colors on the graph.
 6. Discuss the results of their trials.
 7. Next, show the students how they will show their data in a different way.

2. Demonstrate command of the conventions of standard English capitalization, punctuation, and spelling when writing.

Knowledge of Language

3. Apply knowledge of language to understand how language functions in different contexts, to make effective choices for meaning or style, and to comprehend more fully when reading or listening.

Vocabulary Acquisition and Use

4. Determine or clarify the meaning of unknown and multiple-meaning words and phrases by using context clues, analyzing meaningful word parts, and consulting general and specialized reference materials, as appropriate.

5. Demonstrate understanding of figurative language, word relationships, and nuances in word meanings.

6. Acquire and use accurately a range of general academic and domain-specific words and phrases sufficient for reading, writing, speaking, and listening at the college and career readiness level; demonstrate independence in gathering vocabulary knowledge when encountering an unknown term important to comprehension or expression.

Mathematical Practices (8)

1. Make sense of problems and persevere in solving them.

2. Reason abstractly and quantitatively.

3. Construct viable arguments and critique the reasoning of others.

4. Model with mathematics.

5. Use appropriate tools strategically.

6. Attend to precision.

7. Look for and make use of structure.

8. Look for and express regularity in repeated reasoning.

Mathematical Content (20)

Counting and Cardinality

- Know number names and the count sequence.
- Count to tell the number of objects.
- Compare numbers.

Operations and Algebraic Thinking

- Represent and solve problems involving addition and subtraction.
- Work with equal groups of objects to gain foundations for multiplication.

8. Review skip counting by 2s.
9. Model how to set up the graph where 1 square is equal to 2. For example, if they had 4 red spins, they would color 2 squares on their graph to represent 4. Review how to show a square and a half square for the number 3.

✎ *Suggested lesson break.*

10. Have the students do the graph again, but this time let 1 square = 2.
11. Allow time to complete the second graph.
12. Discuss doing the graph as a pictograph. Model and show an example of how to do it. The students will next make an exact pictograph of their data. If time allows, have them do the pictograph where 1 image = 2 items.

IV.   Reflect
1. Have students look over the results recorded on the graph. Ask them to see any patterns and think about the number of predictions they got correctly.

IV.   Assessment
Choice 1
Have the students write about the process they did with the lesson and tell what they noticed about their results in relation to probability. They will give examples to support what they wrote from their lesson experience.
Choice 2
Have the students write fractions to show their results and then reduce them.

Extension Activities

1. Do the activity using M&Ms found at these websites and graph the results. (M&Ms lesson http://betterlesson.com/unit/5226/probability?from=tree#/lesson/12206/day-7-m-ms-probability?&_suid=13554294853030241031 5869760995)

(M&Ms response sheet
http://betterlesson.com/unit/5226/probability
?from=tree#/document/57336/d7-mandm
graphsresponse?&_suid=13554294970240130121
1781119126)

2. Have the students make the squares like the ones in the library lesson. Have them choose squares and record their results. Then have them graph the results and identify the fractions that result. Instruct them to do twenty trials and see if they notice a difference.

3. Make a spinner with 5 colors or use a die to test probability. Have them set up the trials and record their results. Have them write about differences or similarities they notice as trials and the amount of choices increase.

4. Do the activity using coin tosses to show heads or tails.

5. After reading the book, have the students write a short description of the main idea of the book. Use the phrase, "I am a mathematician. I know that _____."

Modifications for Grade 1–2

1. Make a simple graphic organizer to use with the spinners.
2. Show the students the colored squares and have them predict what colors will be chosen.
3. Review the four words and practice using them by calling out the situations rather than having the students write them.
4. Make the spinners, and then model what the students will do.
5. Have them record their data for their spins only.
6. Make a class chart.
7. Identify the probability together.
8. Record their results.
9. Lead a discussion about what they noticed in their predictions.

Differentiation strategies:

1. Discuss, define, or review the vocabulary after reading the book. Point out examples of how the words were used in the book.
2. Use strategic grouping for the activity.

- Represent and solve problems involving multiplication and division.
- Multiply and divide within 100 .
- Use the four operations with whole numbers to solve problems.
- Gain familiarity with factors and multiples.
- Write and interpret numerical expressions.
- Analyze patterns and relationships.

Number and Operations in Base Ten

- Understand the place value system.
- Perform operations with multi-digit whole numbers and with decimals to hundredths.

Number and Operations—Fractions

- Develop understanding of fractions as numbers.
- Extend understanding of fraction equivalence and ordering.
- Build fractions from unit fractions by applying and extending previous understandings of operations on whole numbers.
- Use equivalent fractions as a strategy to add and subtract fractions.

Measurement and Data

- Describe and compare measurable attributes.
- Classify objects and count the number of objects in categories.

- Represent and interpret data.

Geometry
- Graph points on the coordinate plane to solve real-world and mathematical problems.

3. Pre-make the spinners to reduce the amount of time needed for the lesson.
4. Reduce the number of spins per student.
5. Have the students record only their own spins.
6. Have the students graph their spins and make a class graph.
7. Repeat the activity, and compare the results.
8. Record each spin in a math sentence to show the probability.

Resources:

Colored spinner
http://www.webeans.net/hutt/educ/colorspinner4.pdf

Black and white spinner
http://www.webeans.net/hutt/educ/spinner4_bw.pdf

M&Ms challenge
http://betterlesson.com/unit/5226/probability?from=tree#/lesson/12206/day-7-m
-ms-probability?&_suid=135542948530302410315869760995

M&Ms response sheet
http://betterlesson.com/unit/5226/probability?from=tree#/document/57336/
d7-mandmgraphsresponse?&_suid=135542949702401301211781119126

Interactive game using the vocabulary words
http://www.kidsmathgamesonline.com/numbers/probability.html

Probability worksheets for kids
http://www.mathworksheets4kids.com/probability.html

More interactive games
http://www.free-training-tutorial.com/probability-games.html

Exemplar Texts:

Bar Graphs.
By Vijaya Khisty Bodach. Capstone, 2008. 32p. (9781429600408)
Grade Level: PreK–2
ATOS Reading Level: 2.1
Lexile Level: AD 400L
Dewey: 510

Football Numbers: Graphing Data.
By John Perritano. Norwood House, 2013. 32p. (978599535661)

Grade Level: 3–5
ATOS Reading Level: 4.2
Lexile Level: 670L
Dewey: 001.4

Let's Make a Bar Graph.
By Robin Nelson. Lerner, 2013. 24p. (9780761389729)
Grade Level: K–2
Lexile Level: 520L
Dewey: 001.4226

The Garden Club: Operations with Fractions.
By Renata Brunner-Jass. Norwood House, 2013. 48p. (9781599535708)
Grade Level: 4–6
ATOS Reading Level: 5.3
Lexile Level: 820L
Dewey: 513.2

Understanding Charts and Graphs.
By Christine Taylor-Butler. Children's Press, 2012. 48p. (9780531260098)
Grade Level: 4–8
ATOS Reading Level: 5.5
Lexile Level: 820L
Dewey: 001.4226

21

For Good Measure: The Ways We Say How Much, How Far, How Heavy, How Big, How Old

By Ken Robbins. Roaring Brook Press, 2010. 48p. (9781596433441)

Grade Level: 3–5 *(Grades 1–2 with modifications)*
ATOS Reading Level: 6.4
Dewey: 530.8
Subject Area: mathematics

Essential Question: Why do people need a standard unit for measuring length and area?

Unit Summary: Students will examine the essential question, "Why do people need a standard unit for measuring length and area?" They will explore measurement by finding the dimensions of a library table using their own feet as a nonstandard unit and record the data to see the variations that result from their measurements. They will develop a data table and record their measuring activity on it. The students will then practice accurately using U.S. standard units with a ruler and yardstick by measuring the table's correct dimensions to find its area. They will compare the differences they have collected

3. Analyze how and why individuals, events, and ideas develop and interact over the course of a text.

Craft and Structure

4. Interpret words and phrases as they are used in a text, including determining technical, connotative, and figurative meanings, and analyze how specific word choices shape meaning or tone.

Integration of Knowledge and Ideas

7. Integrate and evaluate content presented in diverse media and formats, including visually and quantitatively, as well as in words.

8. Delineate and evaluate the argument and specific claims in a text, including the validity of the reasoning as well as the relevance and sufficiency of the evidence.

Range of Reading and Level of Text Complexity

10. Read and comprehend complex literary and informational texts independently and proficiently.

Writing Standards (5)

Text Types and Purposes

2. Write informative/ explanatory texts to examine and convey complex ideas and information clearly and accurately through the effective selection, organization, and analysis of content.

and identify which is the more accurate way to measure items.

Vocabulary: area, century, decade, exact, foot, inch, length, measure, measurement, metric, millennium, perimeter, precise, standard, unit, volume, weight, width, yard

Approximate lesson time: one or two class periods

Booktalk: How much is a lot? Or a few? Words don't always tell you exact amounts. That's why we have units of measure. Of course, they weren't always exact—or even the same! Over time, two standards came about to use for accurately measuring things like weight, distance, and how much is in something, called volume. One system is the metric system. It's based on 10. It's easy to multiply or divide numbers by 10. Much of the world uses this standard. But the standards used in the United States are called U.S. customary units. How did this variety of units develop and how do we use them? Let's take a look at the book *For Good Measure.*

Book Time

1. Share the booktalk for *For Good Measure* (above).
2. Read the introduction and section on lengths and distances.
3. After reading these two sections, review and list the units of measure described in the book in both standard U.S. units and metric units.

Library Activity

What's My Size?

I. Materials: rulers, yardsticks, graphic organizer
II. Instructions
1. Tell the students they will be measuring something in two different ways and comparing them to show how we need a standard unit to talk about measurements.
2. They will begin by measuring the area of one library table surface. However, they will be using one of the original units for measuring area.

3. Have the students remove their shoes.
4. Tell them they will measure the length and width of their library table using their feet like people did long ago. They will record the measurement to the nearest whole foot unit. For example, if the measure is 9 feet and a little, they will record 9 feet. If the measure is 9 feet and almost another 10, they will round up to 10, the next whole number. Then they'll use those measurements to calculate the area of the table top.

III.   Procedure
1. Distribute the graphic organizer for this lesson.
2. Each student will then walk the length of the table (they'll have to pace around the bottom with their feet while keeping their hip against the table top—no walking on top of the table!).
3. Each student how many (student) feet the length is for each person at their table. They will label the feet after rounding to the nearest whole number.

✏ *Suggested lesson break.*

4. Next have students measure the width of the table to the nearest foot and record their own measurements and those of their tablemates.
5. Each student will then multiply the length times the width to calculate the area of the table's surface. You may have to show them or remind them how to express area in square feet.
6. Have the students post their numbers on a group chart.
7. Discuss why the various numbers are different.
8. Now have the students measure the length of one of their own feet in inches. Record the number on their data sheet. Keep this paper to use for an extension activity.

✏ *Suggested lesson break.*

Production and Distribution of Writing

4. Produce clear and coherent writing in which the development, organization, and style are appropriate to task, purpose, and audience.

5. Develop and strengthen writing as needed by planning, revising, editing, rewriting, or trying a new approach.

Research to Build and Present Knowledge

7. Conduct short as well as more sustained research projects based on focused questions, demonstrating understanding of the subject under investigation.

Range of Writing

10. Write routinely over extended time frames (time for research, reflection, and revision) and shorter time frames (a single sitting or a day or two) for a range of tasks, purposes, and audiences.

Speaking and Listening Standards (6)

Comprehension and Collaboration

1. Prepare for and participate effectively in a range of conversations and collaborations with diverse partners, building on others' ideas and expressing their own clearly and persuasively.

2. Integrate and evaluate information presented in diverse media and formats, including visually, quantitatively, and orally.

Presentation of Knowledge and Ideas

4. Present information, findings, and supporting evidence such that listeners can follow the line of reasoning and the organization, development, and style are appropriate to task, purpose, and audience.

5. Make strategic use of digital media and visual displays of data to express information and enhance understanding of presentations.

6. Adapt speech to a variety of contexts and communicative tasks, demonstrating command of formal English when indicated or appropriate.

Language Standards (6)

Conventions of Standard English

1. Demonstrate command of the conventions of standard English grammar and usage when writing or speaking.

2. Demonstrate command of the conventions of standard English capitalization, punctuation, and spelling when writing.

IV. Redo the activity
1. Repeat the table-measuring activity using inches or feet. This time use standard U.S. measurements, rounding to the nearest inch.
2. Calculate the area of the table in standard measures.
3. Compare the answers within their group. The numbers should be the same.
4. Lead a discussion about their results and why standard units developed for measuring things to answer the essential question.

V. Reflect
1. Ask the groups of students to think back over their activity. Have the students tell their group one thing they learned by doing today's activity.
2. Then have them identify something else they could measure to determine the area.

VI. Assessment
Choice 1
Have the students measure a sheet of notebook paper or art paper by length and width. Then have them calculate the area of the paper. Remind them to express their answer in square inches.
Choice 2
Pass out a square and have the students measure it. Then have the students calculate the area of the square. Give each student another square and, in groups, ask them to determine the total area of all the squares at their table.

Collaborative Teacher Activity

Can You Fathom It?

I. Materials: rulers, yardsticks, paper to record measurements
II. Instructions
1. Read and review the fathom section in the book.
2. Ask the students to model a fathom using their own arms.
3. Review the meaning of area and perimeter. Discuss the difference between the two.

Remind them that peRIMeter has the word "rim" in it. Perimeter goes around the rim of something.

4. Have one student model the room's perimeter by walking around the edge of the classroom.
5. Tell them they will be measuring and calculating the area and perimeter of this classroom today.
6. Explain that they will be measuring the area and perimeter both in fathoms and in standard units.
7. Pair up students or put them in small groups.

III. Procedure

1. Ask each student to set up a data page.
2. Have the group members measure the length and width of the classroom in fathoms (their own). Record their measurements and calculate both the area and perimeter in fathoms.
3. Then have the groups work together to measure the length and width of the classroom in inches, rounding to the nearest whole number.
4. Ask one group member from every group to write the two figures on a class chart.
5. Discuss the results.

✐ *Suggested lesson break.*

6. Then have each group measure the length and width of the classroom to the nearest inch, half inch, or quarter inch, depending on the grade level.
7. Compare the rounded length and width to the nearest quarter or half inch measurements.
8. Discuss which measure would provide a more accurate measurement.

IV. Assessment

Choice 1

Give the length and width of a square or rectangular shape or piece of paper. Tell each student to calculate the area and perimeter of the object.

Knowledge of Language

3. Apply knowledge of language to understand how language functions in different contexts, to make effective choices for meaning or style, and to comprehend more fully when reading or listening.

Vocabulary Acquisition and Use

4. Determine or clarify the meaning of unknown and multiple-meaning words and phrases by using context clues, analyzing meaningful word parts, and consulting general and specialized reference materials, as appropriate.

5. Demonstrate understanding of figurative language, word relationships, and nuances in word meanings.

6. Acquire and use accurately a range of general academic and domain-specific words and phrases sufficient for reading, writing, speaking, and listening at the college and career readiness level; demonstrate independence in gathering vocabulary knowledge when encountering an unknown term important to comprehension or expression.

Mathematical Practices (8)

1. Make sense of problems and persevere in solving them.

2. Reason abstractly and quantitatively.

3. Construct viable arguments and critique the reasoning of others.

4. Model with mathematics.

5. Use appropriate tools strategically.

6. Attend to precision.

7. Look for and make use of structure.

8. Look for and express regularity in repeated reasoning.

Mathematical Content (32)

Counting and Cardinality

- Compare numbers.
- Represent and solve problems involving addition and subtraction.

Operations and Algebraic Thinking

- Understand and apply properties of operations and the relationship between addition and subtraction.
- Work with addition and subtraction equations.
- Represent and solve problems involving addition and subtraction.
- Represent and solve problems involving multiplication and division.
- Understand properties of multiplication and the relationship be-

Choice 2

Have students draw a rectangle. They will then label the length and width. Unless you provide a standard rectangle, have the students choose a length and width of a rectangular shape and label it. (If you use a standard size for everyone, have them measure it.) Ask them to then calculate the area and perimeter.

Extension Activities

1. Measure a given rectangle's width and length. Calculate the area in square inches. Then use graph paper with each square representing a square inch. Transfer the rectangle's area onto the graph paper by coloring in the correct number of square inches.
2. Make a bar graph of each individual student's foot measurement to show the variance of the different sizes. Then create addition and subtraction word problems using the data on the graph.
3. Make a list of all the different terms used to measure things. Group the words that measure length, weight, and volume. Then find each word's equivalent in the metric system.
4. After reading the book, have the students write a short description of the main idea of the book. Use the phrase, "I am a mathematician. I know that _____."

Modifications for Grades K–2

1. Model how to measure with a 1-foot ruler and how to add the feet prior to the lesson.
2. Model the activity to show them how to measure using their own foot, the foot of a volunteer, or your own foot.
3. Do the activity using a ruler rather than a yardstick and have the students measure something smaller than a library table, such as a precut set of butcher paper rectangles that can be designed to be closer to whole units.
4. Discuss the two results after measuring both ways and why standard measure is useful.

5. If you wish, have the students calculate the perimeter of your chosen table or paper in a manner similar to the collaborative activity, but use feet rather than inches.

Differentiation strategies:

1. Discuss, define, or review the vocabulary before or after reading the book.
2. Point out examples of how the words were used in the book.
3. Use strategic grouping for the activity.
4. Review how to measure before beginning the library activity.
5. Discuss how to calculate area and perimeter and practice doing so before introducing the lesson.
6. Review rounding numbers to the nearest unit in inches and feet.
7. Practice measuring something smaller or choose a different item to measure.

Resources:

Measuring metric length
http://www.wisc-online.com/objects/ViewObject
.aspx?ID=ABM4202

Measuring in inches—interactive
http://www.softschools.com/measurement/games/
ruler/measuring_length_in_inches/

About measuring length
http://atlantis.coe.uh.edu/archive/science/science_
lessons/scienceles3/length/length.html

Exemplar Texts:

A Day at Mini-Golf: What's the Length?
By Donna Loughran. Norwood House, 2013. 24p.
  (9781599535562)
Grade Level: K–3
ATOS Reading Level: 2.8
Lexile Level: 460L
Dewey: 530.8

How Long Is Long?: Comparing Animals.
By Vic Parker. Heinemann, 2011. 32p. (9781432939588)

tween multiplication and division.
- Multiply and divide within 100.
- Solve problems involving the four operations, and identify and explain patterns in arithmetic.
- Use the four operations with whole numbers to solve problems.
- Generate and analyze patterns.
- Write and interpret numerical expressions.
- Analyze patterns and relationships.

Number and Operations in Base Ten
- Use place value understanding and properties of operations to add and subtract.
- Use place value understanding and properties of operations to perform multi-digit arithmetic.

Number and Operations—Fractions
- Develop understanding of fractions as numbers.
- Extend understanding of fraction equivalence and ordering.
- Build fractions from unit fractions by applying and extending previous understandings of operations on whole numbers.

Measurement and Data
- Describe and compare measurable attributes.

- Classify objects and count the number of objects in categories.
- Measure lengths indirectly and by iterating length units.
- Measure and estimate lengths in standard units.
- Relate addition and subtraction to length.
- Represent and interpret data.
- Geometric measurement: understand concepts of area and relate area to multiplication and to addition.
- Geometric measurement: recognize perimeter as an attribute of plane figures and distinguish between linear and area measures.
- Solve problems involving measurement and conversion of measurements from a larger unit to a smaller unit.
- Convert like measurement units within a given measurement system.

Geometry
- Identify and describe shapes.
- Analyze, compare, create, and compose shapes.
- Reason with shapes and their attributes.
- Classify two-dimensional figures into categories based on their properties.

Grade Level: K–3
Lexile Level: IG 690L
Dewey: 530.8

How Long or How Wide?: A Measuring Guide.
By Brian P. Cleary. Millbrook, 2007. 32p. (9780822566946)
Grade Level: K–3
ATOS Reading Level: 3.1
Lexile Level: 730L
Dewey: 530.8

How Tall? How Wide?
By Cecilia Minden. Cherry Lake, 2011. 24p. (9781602798489)
Grade Level: K–2
Lexile Level: 240L
Dewey: 530.8

Measurement: The Measured Mystery.
By Emily Sohn and Karen Rothbardt. Norwood House, 2011. 32p. (9781599534176)
Grade Level: 3–5
ATOS Reading Level: 3.7
Lexile Level: 510L
Dewey: 530

22

How Many Jelly Beans?

By Andrea Menotti. Chronicle, 2012. 32p. (9781452102061)

Grade Level: K–2 *(Grades 3–5 with modifications)*
ATOS Reading Level: 1.5
Dewey: E
Subject Area: mathematics

Essential Question: What would a million of something look like?

Unit Summary: Students will examine the essential question, "What would a million of something look like?" They will explore numbers of increasing size through the enlarging number of jelly beans pictured in the book. They will color sets of five jelly beans and practice skip counting by five as they complete each row on the graphic organizer. Each student will count the number of jelly beans on each row and label it as five, and then return to the top of the page and skip count by fives, marking each set with a cumulative number. They will use the sets of five to write number sentences and circle groups to make changes in the number sentences. They will recognize their picture of jelly beans as totaling one hundred.

Vocabulary: building, hundred, jelly beans, million, ones, second, stacked, tens, thousand, year

Approximate lesson time: one to two class periods

Booktalk: Think about eating two or three pieces of candy every day. Would that be a good idea? Or even

8. Delineate and evaluate the argument and specific claims in a text, including the validity of the reasoning as well as the relevance and sufficiency of the evidence.

Range of Reading and Level of Text Complexity

10. Read and comprehend complex literary and informational texts independently and proficiently.

Writing Standards (6)

Text Types and Purposes

2. Write informative/explanatory texts to examine and convey complex ideas and information clearly and accurately through the effective selection, organization, and analysis of content.

Production and Distribution of Writing

4. Produce clear and coherent writing in which the development, organization, and style are appropriate to task, purpose, and audience.

Research to Build and Present Knowledge

7. Conduct short as well as more sustained research projects based on focused questions, demonstrating understanding of the subject under investigation.

8. Gather relevant information from multiple print and digital sources, assess

healthy? Counting candy is what this book is about, and the children in it try to top one another in the size of large numbers. How many is one million? Can you count to one million? Have you ever seen a million things? Today you will. Let's take a look at this book and see what kind of giant numbers we can find.

Book Time

1. Share the booktalk for *How Many Jelly Beans* (above).
2. Read the book straight through.
3. Allow time for the students to look at the million page. A magnifying glass will provide a better perspective of the dots representing one million.
4. Reread the book. Stop to count the low number of jelly beans and point out the larger number of jelly beans. *For short library periods, skip activity four.

 Library Activity

Jelly Bean Math

I. Materials: crayons, pencils, jelly beans to share (optional), graphic organizer (or large drawing paper if you prefer the students draw their own images)

II. Instructions
   1. Tell the students they will be counting and coloring jelly beans to show skip counting and to see how larger numbers are expressed.
   2. They will show the number 100 represented by jelly beans they color. Tell them they will make their number 100 in rows by fives. They'll practice skip counting and see how numbers add together to make 100.

III. Procedure
   1. Give each student a copy of the graphic organizer.
   2. Before the students begin work, model the array they will be drawing and labeling. Draw the jelly beans large or project the graphic organizer. Tell them they will work in rows of five. Go down the page, coloring five jelly beans at a time. Each jelly bean

has to be a different color than the ones on either side of each one. For example, they can't color a jelly bean red and then color the one next to it red, too. Alternatively, you might have them color 5 jelly beans all the same color to indicate the sets of 5.

3. Have them continue moving down the page by 5s, coloring in their jelly beans.

4. When they have completed the 20 rows of jelly beans, they stop. Return to the top of their page and count the number of jelly beans in the first row. Then write down the numeral 5 *in front* of that row. Continue down the page with the counting and the numeral 5. They'll be labeling the number 5 to the column left of their images. Continue down the page until each row is labeled 5.

✎ *Suggested lesson break.*

5. Next, have them return to the top and count the first row again. There will be five. Write the number 5 *to the right* of the row of images. Then have them continue counting after five to include the next row. That number will be 10. Have them write 10 *at the end* of that row.

6. Continue down the page adding the numbers of 5 each time so that the finished count shows skip counting by 5s. The right side of their page will reflect 5, 10, 15, 20, etc. Have them practice skip counting by 5s by reading their numbers to a partner.

7. Then ask them to write a number sentence to show their picture. They may write "5 + 5 + 5" and so on until they have 20 fives written and that = 100. They might combine rows, too. Accept any correct answers.

8. Next have them circle two lines of 5s all the way down the page to make new groups. Practice skip counting by 10s to 100.

9. Collect the papers so the collaborating teacher can use them in the next lesson.

10. Discuss the essential question and their reaction to seeing 1,000,000 dots representing jelly beans.

the credibility and accuracy of each source, and integrate the information while avoiding plagiarism.

9. Draw evidence from literary or informational texts to support analysis, reflection, and research.

Range of Writing

10. Write routinely over extended time frames (time for research, reflection, and revision) and shorter time frames (a single sitting or a day or two) for a range of tasks, purposes, and audiences.

Speaking and Listening Standards (5)

Comprehension and Collaboration

1. Prepare for and participate effectively in a range of conversations and collaborations with diverse partners, building on others' ideas and expressing their own clearly and persuasively.

2. Integrate and evaluate information presented in diverse media and formats, including visually, quantitatively, and orally.

Presentation of Knowledge and Ideas

4. Present information, findings, and supporting evidence such that listeners can follow the line of reasoning and the organization, development, and

style are appropriate to task, purpose, and audience.

5. Make strategic use of digital media and visual displays of data to express information and enhance understanding of presentations.

6. Adapt speech to a variety of contexts and communicative tasks, demonstrating command of formal English when indicated or appropriate.

Language Standards (4)

Conventions of Standard English

1. Demonstrate command of the conventions of standard English grammar and usage when writing or speaking.

2. Demonstrate command of the conventions of standard English capitalization, punctuation, and spelling when writing.

Knowledge of Language

3. Apply knowledge of language to understand how language functions in different contexts, to make effective choices for meaning or style, and to comprehend more fully when reading or listening.

Vocabulary Acquisition and Use

6. Acquire and use accurately a range of general

IV. Reflect
1. Have the students pair up and share their jelly bean pictures. Then have them skip count by 10s and by 5s to one another.
2. Ask them to look at their page. See if they can find one more number sentence. Ask volunteers to share their number sentence with the class and discuss their ideas.

VI. Assessment
Choice 1
Provide a paper with 100 circles or other images. Ask the students to group them and then write a number sentence to show their grouping.
Choice 2
Have the students make their own images by 5s or 10s and write a number sentence to show three ways it can be grouped.

Collaborative Teacher Activity

Sharing Jelly Beans

I. Materials: paper, crayons, pencils, jelly beans (optional)

II. Instructions
1. Review the book by reading to the class. At each number, stop and write in a prominent place the number being discussed. For example, begin with 10, 20, 25, 50, and so on until one million. As you write, put them in the proper place value.
2. After the book ends, ask the students if they see any patterns in the numbers. Discuss their observations.
3. Return to the pages in the book near the end where the hundred thousand jelly beans are broken down into the different flavors. Write those numbers near the first set of numbers and then add them. Talk about how they add up to 100,000. Tell the students they are going to break up their numbers in the same way—except they'll work with 100.

III. Procedure
1. Review place value up to the 100s place and the significance of 10 ones and 10 tens.

2. Pass out the student papers from the library lesson. Review what they did and put them aside.

3. Tell the students they will break down their 100 jelly beans into groups or multiples of 10. They will make a picture of something like the pages from the book, but they will only go to 100.

4. Practice skip counting by 10s.

5. Tell them they will draw jelly beans in groups of 10 and will color in multiples of 10 to add up to 100. Instruct them that every circle can't have only 10 in it; some of them must be larger numbers, like 20 or 40.

6. Tell the students it might be easier to draw the group of jelly beans first and then put the circle around them. Tell them the circles don't have to be perfect and show them the book pages again.

7. Allow time for the students to work on their jelly bean pictures. You might want them to break down their larger number by putting it into rows of 10s inside the circle.

8. Next have them write a number sentence that shows their work. Ask if they can write short number sentences and then add those together.

9. When everyone is finished, have the students form a circle around the room. Go around the circle and have each student hold up their paper and state the number to skip count by 100s. For example, the first child will say 100, the second child will say 200, and so on. Stop at 900 and discuss what number will be next. Continue counting until every student has added in their 100 jelly beans, and then have them return to their seats and show the final number where everyone can see it.

🖉 *Suggested lesson break.*

10. Then model how to subtract from 100. Have the students use their library paper to cover one circle of jelly beans and count the remaining ones by 10. Give the answer. Then ask

academic and domain-specific words and phrases sufficient for reading, writing, speaking, and listening at the college and career readiness level; demonstrate independence in gathering vocabulary knowledge when encountering an unknown term important to comprehension or expression.

Mathematical Practices (8)

1. Make sense of problems and persevere in solving them.

2. Reason abstractly and quantitatively.

3. Construct viable arguments and critique the reasoning of others.

4. Model with mathematics.

5. Use appropriate tools strategically.

6. Attend to precision.

7. Look for and make use of structure.

8. Look for and express regularity in repeated reasoning.

Mathematical Content (20)

Counting and Cardinality
- Know number names and the count sequence.
- Count to tell the number of objects.
- Compare numbers.

Operations and Algebraic Thinking

- Understand addition as putting together and adding to, and understand subtraction as taking apart and taking from.
- Represent and solve problems involving addition and subtraction.
- Understand and apply properties of operations and the relationship between addition and subtraction.
- Work with addition and subtraction equations.
- Add and subtract within 20.
- Work with equal groups of objects to gain foundations for multiplication.
- Represent and solve problems involving multiplication and division.
- Understand properties of multiplication and the relationship between multiplication and division.
- Multiply and divide within 100.
- Solve problems involving the four operations, and identify and explain patterns in arithmetic.
- Write and interpret numerical expressions.
- Analyze patterns and relationships.

Number and Operations in Base Ten

- Extend the counting sequence.

them to cover two circles and find the remainder. Have them write the problems as number sentences.

11. Then have the students do the same activity with their new work. Model with one student's paper and write the corresponding number sentence. Then have the students write more number sentences using subtraction.

IV. Reflect
1. Have the students turn to a partner and read them the number sentence they made. Then ask each one to point it out on their paper.
2. Have each student re-count the jelly beans on his or her own paper and look it over. Ask them to think about another way they might have shown numbers to 100.

IV. Assessment
Choice 1
Give the students a page with rectangles in rows and columns of 5s. Have them circle any groups they see and write a number sentence to show their circles.
Choice 2
Have the students draw 5 rows and columns of jelly beans. Have them group the rows and columns using circles and write number sentences to show their groupings.

Extension Activities

1. Give each student ten jelly beans or ten bite-sized candies. Have them write story problems and the number sentences using subtraction as they eat them.
2. Give each student a 100-box grid. Have them write the numbers to 100. Then shade in the square to form a picture. Have them write the number and break it down into the place value of the shaded squares. For example, if 76 had been shaded, they would write: "76 = 7 tens and 6 ones"; they would continue with the other numbers they had shaded. Take up the papers and use some of them to make a mystery picture activity. See an example here:

http://thefirstgradeparade.blogspot.com/ 2011/01/place-value-mystery-pictures.html.

Use the grid with 100 marked on it and by using the clues (7 tens and 6 ones = ?), the class will shade in the numbers to see the picture.

3. Bring in a package of beans or peas. Ask the students how many beans are in the package. Then give a handful to each person until they are all distributed. Ask them to count their beans and write it down. Then have the students make piles of 10 and re-count the beans. Ask which way is easier. Count the beans by 10s for everyone in the class to get the total number of beans. Then take a set amount of beans and write number sentences. You can do this with numbers up to 20 to review addition and subtraction or make larger numbers. Group the students and have them work together with more beans.

4. After reading the book, have the students write a short description of the main idea of the book. Use the phrase, "I am a mathematician. I know that _____."

- Use place value understanding and properties of operations to perform multi-digit arithmetic.

Measurement and Data
- Describe and compare measurable attributes.
- Classify objects and count the number of objects in categories.
- Represent and interpret data.

Modifications for Grade 3

1. Use the numbers from the book up to 1,000 to multiply by 10 to show the progression of size when multiplied in 10s.
2. Write number sentences that show the pattern. Begin with 1 x 10, 2 x 10, 3 x 10, etc. and then go on to 100 x 10 to illustrate the point that multiplying by 10 will increase the number of zeroes.
3. Continue with 1 x 10, 10 x 10, and 100 x 10. See how far they can continue using the pattern and practice using it.

Modifications for Grade 4

1. Use the numbers from the book up to 1,000 to multiply by 10 to show the progression of size when multiplied in 10s.
2. Write number sentences that show the pattern.
3. Then take a multi-digit number and write number sentences to show greater than, less than, and equal.

Modifications for Grade 5

1. Use the principle of multiples of 10 to review decimals and practice multiplying whole numbers and decimals by 10.

Differentiation strategies:

1. Discuss, define, or review the vocabulary after reading the book. Point out examples of how the words were used in the book.
2. Use strategic grouping for the activity.

3. Have your group draw the jelly beans for the activity rather than using the graphic organizer.
4. Review place value and draw a place value chart ahead of time for the students to fill in using 1, 10, 100, 1,000, and so on to use as a reference.
5. Check with the math teacher for the level the students in each grade have progressed to and work within those numbers.
6. Color each set of five jelly beans the same color to show the sets of five.

Resources:

Review of place value and chart to 100 billions
http://www.mathatube.com/place-value-charts.html

Place value that includes decimals
http://www.enchantedlearning.com/math/decimals/placevalue/

Breakdown of place value in numbers
http://www.helpingwithmath.com/printables/tables_charts/cha0301place_value
   _thousands01.htm

Interactive place value game
http://www.wmnet.org.uk/wmnet/custom/files_uploaded/uploaded
   _resources/853/PlaceValueChartv4.swf

Exemplar Texts:

Ants at the Picnic: Counting by Tens.
By Michael Dahl. Picture Window Books, 2006. 24p. (9781404813182)
Grade Level: PreK–2
ATOS Reading Level: 1.6
Lexile Level: AD 260L
Dewey: 513.2

Busy Beavers: Counting by 5s.
By Megan Atwood. Magic Wagon, 2012. 24p. (9781616418526)
Grade Level: PreK–2
ATOS Reading Level: 2.7
Dewey: 513.2

Tally Cat Keeps Track.
By Trudy Harris. Millbrook Press, 2011. 32p. (9780761344513)
Grade Level: K–3
ATOS Reading Level: 3.1
Lexile Level: 570L
Dewey: E

Toy Tally: How Many Toys Are There?
By Donna Loughran. Norwood House, 2013. 24p. (9781599535531)
Grade Level: K–3
ATOS Reading Level: 3.0
Lexile Level: 480L
Dewey: 513.2

Winning the Game: Putting Miles in Their Place.
By Renata Brunner-Jass. Norwood House, 2013. 48p. (9781599535678)
Grade Level: 4–6
ATOS Reading Level: 3.9
Lexile Level: 620L
Dewey: 513.5

 **23**

Infinity and Me

By Kate Hosford. Carolrhoda Books, 2012. 32p. (9780761367260)

Grade Level: 3–5 *(Grades K–2 with modifications)*
ATOS Reading Level: 3.4
Lexile Level: AD 670L (Adult Directed)
Dewey: E
Subject Area: mathematics, science

Essential Question: "What is infinity?"

Unit Summary: Students will examine the essential question, "What is infinity?" The students will use a strand of a cooked spaghetti noodle to help them visualize the concept. Each student will fold the strand of spaghetti in half and make a cut to divide it into two equal pieces. They will measure the half and record its length to the nearest 1/8 inch on their data table. Then they will repeat the step, cutting the half into a half and measuring its length until they can no longer measure the strand. They will cut the remaining piece as small as possible until they can no longer make a cut. After observing their data, the students will discuss infinity and state their own idea about the concept of infinity.

Vocabulary: billion, endless, forever, infinity, million, music, noodle, racetrack, recess, spices, symbol

Approximate lesson time: one to two class periods

Booktalk: How big is infinity? Have you ever said that something is as much or as big as infinity? Or used the phrase "infinity times infinity"? Sometimes it's hard to picture something that never ends. Is there a way to talk

Common Core State Standards (65 total)

Reading Standards (7)

Key Ideas and Details

1. Read closely to determine what the text says explicitly and to make logical inferences from it; cite specific textual evidence when writing or speaking to support conclusions drawn from the text.

2. Determine central ideas or themes of a text and analyze their development; summarize the key supporting details and ideas.

3. Analyze how and why individuals, events, and ideas develop and interact over the course of a text.

Craft and Structure

4. Interpret words and phrases as they are used in a text, including determining technical, connotative, and figurative meanings, and analyze how specific

word choices shape meaning or tone.

Integration of Knowledge and Ideas

7. Integrate and evaluate content presented in diverse media and formats, including visually and quantitatively, as well as in words.

8. Delineate and evaluate the argument and specific claims in a text, including the validity of the reasoning as well as the relevance and sufficiency of the evidence.

Range of Reading and Level of Text Complexity

10. Read and comprehend complex literary and informational texts independently and proficiently.

Writing Standards (7)

Text Types and Purposes

2. Write informative/ explanatory texts to examine and convey complex ideas and information clearly and accurately through the effective selection, organization, and analysis of content.

3. Write narratives to develop real or imagined experiences or events using effective technique, well-chosen details, and well-structured event sequences.

Production and Distribution of Writing

4. Produce clear and coherent writing in which

about infinity and describe it? What exactly is infinity? Let's take a look at the book *Infinity and Me* and see what it says and maybe you can get a better idea of the size of infinity.

Book Time

1. Share the booktalk for *Infinity and Me* (above).
2. Discuss the different ways the book described infinity. List them where everyone can see the examples.
3. Reread the first full spread and the last page. Talk about how Uma felt about infinity on the first spread of the book compared to how she felt on the final page of the book.

 Library Activity

Spaghetti Infinity

I. Materials: long strands of cooked spaghetti noodles, rulers down to 1/8 inch, plastic knives, rolls of waxed paper or paper towels (one square per student), graphic organizer

II. Instructions
　1. Tell the students they will be trying out Mr. Mancini's idea of infinity and that you'll re-read the two pages where Uma tries it out.
　2. Tell them they will cut a spaghetti noodle after they measure it, and keep cutting it as far as possible. They will be measuring each cut they make to the nearest 1/8 inch and recording their data on the graphic organizer. You may want to use a larger fraction for grade 3.

III. Procedure
　1. Pass out one cooked spaghetti strand to each student.
　2. Give the students their graphic organizer. Tell them they will be cutting their spaghetti strands in half and ask them to visualize how many cuts they think it will take to get so small they can't cut it any smaller. Tell them to make a mark to show where they think they will have to stop cutting.
　3. Measure the original length of the spaghetti. Record the length to the nearest 1/8 inch on the data table.

4. Fold the spaghetti strand in half. Make a cut through the half so that both strands are exactly equal. Measure and record the data for the first cut, which would be one half.

5. Continue folding, cutting, and measuring until the spaghetti is too small to fold. Each time, they record the length of the half on their data table.

6. When the strand is less than 1/8 inch, have them try to keep cutting, but stop measuring. Tell them to picture in their minds as they cut how they could continue cutting the spaghetti to infinity.

✎ *Suggested lesson break.*

7. Ask the students to share their data in pairs. Have them notice the differences in the starting lengths.

8. Lead a discussion about the activity and ask what the students noticed. Include talking about the starting lengths of the different spaghetti strands and how differing lengths affected their measurements compared to other students.

9. Ask the students to answer the essential question by writing down their idea of infinity.

IV.   Reflect

1. Have the students arrange their cut halves down the waxed paper or paper towels to create a pattern that illustrates the descending sizes of the pieces.

2. Talk about what they noticed in the pattern in small groups.

VI.   Assessment

Choice 1

Have the students use their spaghetti pattern and data table to write five equations that illustrate five sections of the spaghetti. For example, a student may write "6 ½ inches + 6 ½ inches = 13 inches."

Choice 2

Ask the students to write about their experience and describe their own definition of infinity. Tell them that they can't use anything that was described in the book.

the development, organization, and style are appropriate to task, purpose, and audience.

5. Develop and strengthen writing as needed by planning, revising, editing, rewriting, or trying a new approach.

Research to Build and Present Knowledge

7. Conduct short as well as more sustained research projects based on focused questions, demonstrating understanding of the subject under investigation.

9. Draw evidence from literary or informational texts to support analysis, reflection, and research.

Range of Writing

10. Write routinely over extended time frames (time for research, reflection, and revision) and shorter time frames (a single sitting or a day or two) for a range of tasks, purposes, and audiences.

Speaking and Listening Standards (5)

Comprehension and Collaboration

1. Prepare for and participate effectively in a range of conversations and collaborations with diverse partners, building on others' ideas and expressing their own clearly and persuasively.

2. Integrate and evaluate information presented in diverse media and formats, including visually, quantitatively, and orally.

Presentation of Knowledge and Ideas

4. Present information, findings, and supporting evidence such that listeners can follow the line of reasoning and the organization, development, and style are appropriate to task, purpose, and audience.

5. Make strategic use of digital media and visual displays of data to express information and enhance understanding of presentations.

6. Adapt speech to a variety of contexts and communicative tasks, demonstrating command of formal English when indicated or appropriate.

Language Standards (6)

Conventions of Standard English

1. Demonstrate command of the conventions of standard English grammar and usage when writing or speaking.

2. Demonstrate command of the conventions of standard English capitalization, punctuation, and spelling when writing.

 Collaborative Teacher Activity

Spaghetti Math

I. Materials: rulers, three or four strands of cooked spaghetti noodles per student (make them stronger by cooking them a shorter time than on the directions), waxed paper or paper towels, paper for recording equations

II. Instructions

1. Review the vocabulary related to fractions. Discuss how fractions represent the concept of infinity and relate fractions to the library activity.

2. Tell the students they will be comparing fractions with unlike denominators and decomposing fractions into sums in different ways using spaghetti to illustrate the sums. Remind them that measuring to 1/8 inch is a form of using fractions and show the relationship with examples.

III. Procedure

1. Take three strings of spaghetti and stretch them out side by side. Cut the longer strands so that all strands are exactly the same length. You may want to have everyone measure and cut their strands to 9 inches for easy division into thirds in the next step. Ask them to keep a paper with their measurements.

2. Measure and cut the length of the first strand into halves. Lay the two strands across the top of the desk. Ask the students to write an equation that reflects the two separate parts put together. They might write "½ + ½ = 1." Then ask them to measure the two halves and write another kind of equation. For example, if the strand measured 9 inches, the two halves would measure 4½ inches each. 4½ + 4½ = 9 inches.

3. Have the students try to write the equation a second way. They might use "4 + 4 + ½ + ½ = 8 + ²/₂ = 8 + 1 = 9."

4. Then take the second strand of spaghetti and cut it into thirds. Lay the pieces out

and write a fraction equation to show what the three parts represent.

5. Then have the students write a greater than and less than number sentence to compare the half and the third.

6. Measure and cut the third strand of spaghetti into fourths. Measure and record those lengths. Then have them write equations with halves and fourths.

7. Next, cut the fourths into eighths. Use these lengths to illustrate and write number sentence to show the different varieties of decomposition. Add in the actual lengths to their number sentences if you'd like to.

8. Have the students continue cutting the fourths into eights, and then into sixteenths, and so on. Then have them write the continued numbers down ten more places lower. Share their answers.

IV. Reflect

1. Have the students pair up and demonstrate their number sentences to one another. Ask them to add one new number sentence to their list.

IV. Assessment

Choice 1

Have the students put away their number sentences and have them write new ones using the cut spaghetti strands that reflect what they've practiced in class.

Choice 2

Write about what they've learned from the spaghetti lesson and explain how fractions can be made smaller and smaller and relate that idea to infinity.

Extension Activities

1. Have the students write a story that includes number sentences with fractions and the word "infinity."

2. Look up the symbol for pi and write down what it represents. Then look up this site: http://www.piday.org/million.php. Have the students write several lines of pi's value.

3. After reading the book, have the students write a short description of the main idea of the book.

Knowledge of Language

3. Apply knowledge of language to understand how language functions in different contexts, to make effective choices for meaning or style, and to comprehend more fully when reading or listening.

Vocabulary Acquisition and Use

4. Determine or clarify the meaning of unknown and multiple-meaning words and phrases by using context clues, analyzing meaningful word parts, and consulting general and specialized reference materials, as appropriate.

5. Demonstrate understanding of figurative language, word relationships, and nuances in word meanings.

6. Acquire and use accurately a range of general academic and domain-specific words and phrases sufficient for reading, writing, speaking, and listening at the college and career readiness level; demonstrate independence in gathering vocabulary knowledge when encountering an unknown term important to comprehension or expression.

Mathematical Practices (8)

1. Make sense of problems and persevere in solving them.

2. Reason abstractly and quantitatively.

3. Construct viable arguments and critique the reasoning of others.

4. Model with mathematics.

5. Use appropriate tools strategically.

6. Attend to precision.

7. Look for and make use of structure.

8. Look for and express regularity in repeated reasoning.

Mathematical Content (34)

Counting and Cardinality

- Know number names and the count sequence.
- Count to tell the number of objects.
- Compare numbers.

Operations and Algebraic Thinking

- Understand addition as putting together and adding to, and understand subtraction as taking apart and taking from.
- Represent and solve problems involving addition and subtraction.
- Understand and apply properties of operations and the relationship between addition and subtraction.
- Work with equal groups of objects to gain foun-

Use the phrase, "I am a mathematician. I know that _____."

Modifications for Grades K–2

1. Pass out the strands of spaghetti and have the students measure and cut it to an equal length so that everyone will start with the same sized strand. You might want to use 6 or 8 inches so the halves will be whole numbers.
2. Reread the pages where Uma tries out Mr. Mancini's idea of infinity.
3. Show the students how to fold the strand in half to cut it. Cut the strands and measure the half. Check to see if everyone measured the strand correctly.
4. Discuss what will happen if you continued cutting the spaghetti and describe the cutting if you continued to infinity.
5. Relate the cuts to a number sentence. For example, $\frac{1}{2} + \frac{1}{2} = 1$.
6. Together, have the students cut one of the halves in half. Measure one of the newly cut sections.
7. Ask the students to give you a number sentence and write it where everyone can see it.
8. Relate the numbers to fractions.
9. Then have the students try to cut their remaining halves to infinity.
10. Discuss their results.

Differentiation strategies:

1. Discuss, define, or review pertinent vocabulary after reading the book.
2. Use strategic grouping for the activity or have the students work in pairs.
3. Have the students round their cuts to the nearest quarter or half-inch.
4. Ask the students to form an equivalent fraction for each measure, make it a mixed fraction, or convert it to an improper fraction.
5. Review measuring before starting the activity.
6. Use metric lengths for measuring.

7. Measure units in metric and standard units and discuss which method was easier to work with.

Resources:

One million digits of pi
http://www.piday.org/million.php

Good resource for educators about infinity
http://www.ccs3.lanl.gov/mega-math/workbk/
infinity/inbkgd.html

Number line for explaining infinity
http://www.ccs3.lanl.gov/mega-math/workbk/
infinity/inbkgd.html

Story about infinity
http://www.c3.lanl.gov/mega-math/workbk/infinity/
inhotel.html

Concepts about infinity
http://www.mathacademy.com/pr/minitext/infinity/
index.asp#intro

Exemplar Texts:

A Fraction's Goal: Parts of a Whole.
By Brian P. Cleary. Millbrook Press, 2011. 32p.
   (9780822578819)
Grade Level: K–5
Lexile Level: 620L
Dewey: 513.26

Ivy Sue Needs A House: Building with Equivalent Fractions.
By John Perritano. Norwood House, 2013. 32p.
   (9781599535593)
Grade Level: 3–5
ATOS Reading Level: 3.8
Lexile Level: 640L
Dewey: 513.2

Older Than the Stars.
By Karen C. Fox. Charlesbridge, 2010. 32p.
   (9781570917875)
Grade Level: 2–6
ATOS Reading Level: 5.6
Lexile Level: AD 800L
Dewey: 523.1

dations for multiplication.
- Represent and solve problems involving multiplication and division.
- Understand properties of multiplication and the relationship between multiplication and division.
- Solve problems involving the four operations, and identify and explain patterns in arithmetic.
- Gain familiarity with factors and multiples.
- Generate and analyze patterns.
- Write and interpret numerical expressions.
- Analyze patterns and relationships.

Number and Operations in Base Ten
- Work with numbers 11–19 to gain foundations for place value.
- Extend the counting sequence.
- Understand place value.
- Use place value understanding and properties of operations to add and subtract.
- Use place value understanding and properties of operations to perform multi-digit arithmetic.

Number and Operations—Fractions
- Develop understanding of fractions as numbers.
- Extend understanding of fraction equivalence and ordering.

- Build fractions from unit fractions by applying and extending previous understandings of operations on whole numbers.
- Use equivalent fractions as a strategy to add and subtract fractions.
- Apply and extend previous understandings of multiplication and division to multiply and divide fractions.

Measurement and Data

- Describe and compare measurable attributes.
- Classify objects and count the number of objects in categories.
- Measure lengths indirectly and by iterating length units.
- Measure and estimate lengths in standard units.
- Relate addition and subtraction to length.
- Solve problems involving measurement and conversion of measurements from a larger unit to a smaller unit.
- Represent and interpret data.

Geometry

- Identify and describe shapes.
- Analyze, compare, create, and compose shapes.
- Reason with shapes and their attributes.

Stars Beneath Your Bed: The Surprising Story of Dust.
By April Pulley Sayre. Greenwillow Books, 2005. 32p. (9780060571887)
Grade Level: PreK–4
ATOS Reading Level: 4.6
Lexile Level: AD 640L
Dewey: 551.5113

Tending the Tide Pool: The Parts Make a Whole.
By Donna Loughran. Norwood House, 2013. 24p. (9781599535555)
Grade Level: K–3
ATOS Reading Level: 2.9
Lexile Level: 460L
Dewey: 513.2

24

Missing Math: A Number Mystery

By Loreen Leedy. Marshall Cavendish, 2008. 32p. (9780761453857)

Grade Level: K–3 *(Grades 4–5 with modifications)*
ATOS Reading Level: 2.7
Lexile Level: 460L
Dewey: E
Subject Area: mathematics, reading

Essential Question: Why are numbers important?

Unit Summary: Students will examine the essential question, "Why are numbers important?" They will work in groups to locate numbers from five books from an assigned section of the library based on the Dewey Decimal System. The groups will find books holding specified number criteria and will fill out a chart to show the numbers they have located. They will use their numbers in number sentences to show greater and less than statements. Then students will discuss the value of numbers and ways they use numbers every day.

Vocabulary: amounts, average, calculate, case, clocks, coins, count, emergency, estimate, infinity, multiply, numberless, odd, operate, price, problems, quantities, remotes, scores, temperature, votes, weigh

Approximate lesson time: one to two class periods

Common Core State Standards (57 total)

Reading Standards (7)

Key Ideas and Details

1. Read closely to determine what the text says explicitly and to make logical inferences from it; cite specific textual evidence when writing or speaking to support conclusions drawn from the text.

2. Determine central ideas or themes of a text and analyze their development; summarize the key supporting details and ideas.

3. Analyze how and why individuals, events, and ideas develop and interact over the course of a text.

Craft and Structure

4. Interpret words and phrases as they are used in

a text, including determining technical, connotative, and figurative meanings, and analyze how specific word choices shape meaning or tone.

Integration of Knowledge and Ideas

7. Integrate and evaluate content presented in diverse media and formats, including visually and quantitatively, as well as in words.

8. Delineate and evaluate the argument and specific claims in a text, including the validity of the reasoning as well as the relevance and sufficiency of the evidence.

Range of Reading and Level of Text Complexity

10. Read and comprehend complex literary and informational texts independently and proficiently.

Writing Standards (5)

Text Types and Purposes

2. Write informative/ explanatory texts to examine and convey complex ideas and information clearly and accurately through the effective selection, organization, and analysis of content.

Production and Distribution of Writing

4. Produce clear and coherent writing in which the development, organization, and style are

Booktalk: Think about the numbers you use every day. What time do you get up to go to school? How old are you? What is your telephone number? Most people probably don't think too much about all the ways they use numbers every day, but they'd certainly notice if they didn't have numbers! What might happen if all the numbers disappeared? Let's take a look at the book *Missing Math: A Number Mystery* and find out what might happen.

Book Time

1. Share the booktalk for *Missing Math: A Number Mystery* (above).
2. Discuss the different things in the book that were missing numbers. Make a list as the students name them and post it where everyone can see.
3. Go back and read the book page by page. After each page, add any ways the numbers were missing to the class list.

 Library Activity

Number Detectives

I. Materials: printed copies of the graphic organizer, library books on the shelf, paper and pencils, graphic organizer
II. Instructions
   1. Tell the students they will be number detectives today and they will be looking for their numbers in the library.
   2. Divide the class into seven or eight groups. Assign each group a section of nonfiction according to the Dewey Decimal System. For example, one group would have 100s–199s; another group might have 700s–799s.
   3. Tell them that as number detectives they will be searching for numbers in their section of the library. Each person in the group will be writing, but they'll work together in small groups to locate the books with their numbers.
   4. Ask if anyone knows the meaning of digit. Then define digit: any of the numerals from 1 to 10 and sometimes 0.

III. Procedure

1. Explain to the groups that they will be looking for five different books for the number section they have been assigned and that they will track down what their number in the nonfiction section represents or is about. Introduce the system of classification in the library briefly or review it.

2. Discuss the graphic organizer and what they will look for in the section where they will search. Show a couple of examples, such as page numbers or another easy-to-find number. Explain the list but don't give away any other places to look. Remind them they'll be looking only at books in their assigned section.

3. Tell the students that after working together to find the five books, they will fill in the title, author, and where they found the numbers on each book.

4. Allow time for the students to go to their section and locate the five books they need and record the necessary information.

🖉 *Suggested lesson break.*

5. Discuss where the students found numbers in the library. Then have each group choose two of their numbers from the listed five.

6. Have one group volunteer to share their numbers. Ask them which number is greater and which one is less. Model the number sentence to review greater than and less than to show the students how to write it correctly.

7. Instruct the groups to write five number sentences using their own numbers. Each person will write the number sentences, but they may work together within their group.

8. Allow time for the groups to write and then have each group share a number sentence.

9. Lead a discussion about why numbers are important in books. Then connect the way books are grouped in the collection and how it helps them locate books. Have the students look over their books and see if they can identify the subject their section represents.

appropriate to task, purpose, and audience.

Research to Build and Present Knowledge

7. Conduct short as well as more sustained research projects based on focused questions, demonstrating understanding of the subject under investigation.

9. Draw evidence from literary or informational texts to support analysis, reflection, and research.

Range of Writing

10. Write routinely over extended time frames (time for research, reflection, and revision) and shorter time frames (a single sitting or a day or two) for a range of tasks, purposes, and audiences.

Speaking and Listening Standards (6)

Comprehension and Collaboration

1. Prepare for and participate effectively in a range of conversations and collaborations with diverse partners, building on others' ideas and expressing their own clearly and persuasively.

2. Integrate and evaluate information presented in diverse media and formats, including visually, quantitatively, and orally.

3. Evaluate a speaker's point of view, reasoning, and use of evidence and rhetoric.

Presentation of Knowledge and Ideas

4. Present information, findings, and supporting evidence such that listeners can follow the line of reasoning and the organization, development, and style are appropriate to task, purpose, and audience.

5. Make strategic use of digital media and visual displays of data to express information and enhance understanding of presentations.

6. Adapt speech to a variety of contexts and communicative tasks, demonstrating command of formal English when indicated or appropriate.

Language Standards (6)

Conventions of Standard English

1. Demonstrate command of the conventions of standard English grammar and usage when writing or speaking.

2. Demonstrate command of the conventions of standard English capitalization, punctuation, and spelling when writing.

Knowledge of Language

3. Apply knowledge of language to understand

10. Collect their lists and work to use with the collaborating teacher.
IV. Reflect
   1. Ask each group member to tell the others about why numbers in a library are important.
   2. Each student will tell one way they use numbers outside of school.
VI. Assessment
   Choice 1
      Have the students use their number lists to write two number sentences.
   Choice 2
      Assign the students five numbers and have them write number sentences using greater than and less than symbols.

Collaborative Teacher Activity

Mental Math

I. Materials: paper and pencils
II. Instructions
   1. Tell the students they will be practicing mental math using the numbers they found in the library. They will use those numbers to add and subtract mentally. Discuss what mentally means.
   2. Review skip counting. Have a volunteer count by 10s to 100. Then have the class count aloud by 10s to 100 together. Then ask someone to skip count backwards.
III. Procedure
   1. Choose a multiple of 10 and ask the class what it would be if you added 10 more. For example, if you choose 40, what would the next number be if you counted by 10? Practice by calling out a multiple of 10 and have the students simply write the next number. Check that everyone is catching on and allow time for correcting mistakes.
   2. Then repeat the activity but subtract 10 this time.
   3. Practice the activity, but let the students take turns calling out the multiple of 10. After

each time, check for the correct answer and allow students to make any needed changes.

4. Then repeat the activity, but use multiples of 100. Practice together. Then call out a multiple of 100 and have the students write down the next number for skip counting by 100s.

5. Have a student read out a 3-digit number he or she found in the library lesson. Add 10 mentally and write it down. For example, if the students found 721, their number sentence would be "721 with 10 more = 731." Practice with other numbers and try mentally subtracting 10 as well.

6. Review place value and what each place represents. Break down a 2-digit number and write it in expanded notation. Practice with the students. Then review three places and break down a three-digit number.

7. Using their papers from the library activity, have the students choose one of the numbers and circle it. Ask them to add 10 to that number in their heads. Have them write the number that is 10 larger than their number. Follow up with subtracting 10 from their numbers.

✏ *Suggested lesson break.*

8. Then repeat the activity with a three-digit number. Have them add 100 to their number in their heads and write down the number that is 100 more. Share the answers. Then subtract 100 from their numbers.

9. Model writing the numbers in expanded notation using one of the student numbers.

10. Tell them that they will be writing their five numbers using expanded notation. Have the students work independently or in groups, as needed.

11. Monitor as the students work on their expanded notations.

IV.   Reflect

1. Pair up the students and have them show their partner how they expanded their number. Let them make any corrections and

how language functions in different contexts, to make effective choices for meaning or style, and to comprehend more fully when reading or listening.

Vocabulary Acquisition and Use

4. Determine or clarify the meaning of unknown and multiple-meaning words and phrases by using context clues, analyzing meaningful word parts, and consulting general and specialized reference materials, as appropriate.

5. Demonstrate understanding of figurative language, word relationships, and nuances in word meanings.

6. Acquire and use accurately a range of general academic and domain-specific words and phrases sufficient for reading, writing, speaking, and listening at the college and career readiness level; demonstrate independence in gathering vocabulary knowledge when encountering an unknown term important to comprehension or expression.

Mathematical Practices (8)

1. Make sense of problems and persevere in solving them.

2. Reason abstractly and quantitatively.

3. Construct viable arguments and critique the reasoning of others.

4. Model with mathematics.

5. Use appropriate tools strategically.

6. Attend to precision.

7. Look for and make use of structure.

8. Look for and express regularity in repeated reasoning.

Mathematical Content (25)

Counting and Cardinality

- Know number names and the count sequence.
- Count to tell the number of objects.
- Compare numbers.

Operations and Algebraic Thinking

- Understand and apply properties of operations and the relationship between addition and subtraction.
- Write and interpret numerical expressions.
- Analyze patterns and relationships.
- Use the four operations with whole numbers to solve problems.
- Gain familiarity with factors and multiples.
- Generate and analyze patterns.
- Build fractions from unit fractions by applying and extending

review the rest of their work to see if they think it is correct.

2. Then give the class a number and have one of the pair mentally add 10 to it and tell their partner. Then have the other one in the pair subtract 10 from the number and tell their answer to their partner.

3. Have one member of the pair state a three-digit number and add and subtract 100. Repeat with the other partner.

IV. Assessment

Choice 1

Have the students write out a given three-digit number in expanded notation.

Choice 2

Write about what they've learned about numbers and explain why three-digit numbers are larger than two-digit numbers.

Extension Activities

1. Take a field trip walk around the school. Have the students write down all the numbers they see. Return to class and have them list all the ways numbers are used.

2. Hold a library scavenger hunt. Divide the students into small groups and assign them three numbers that correspond to the call numbers on books in your library. Have them locate books with that number and order them from least to greatest.

4. After reading the book, have the students write a short description of the main idea of the book. Use the phrase, "I am a mathematician. I know that _____."

Modifications for Grades 4–5

1. Do the activity but use mathematics operations suitable for grades 4 and 5, such as multiplying and dividing decimals or large whole numbers.

2. Change the graphic organizer to reflect more difficult numbers.

3. Have the students write out all their numbers in expanded notation form.

4. Increase the number of assigned number sentences.
5. Increase the number of books to find from 5 to 10.

Differentiation strategies:

1. Discuss, define, or review pertinent vocabulary after reading the book.
2. Use strategic grouping for the activity.
3. Present more examples of places in which to find numbers in the books.
4. Increase or decrease the number of books used to locate the numbers.
5. Change the operations to fit the grade doing the lesson.
6. Have the students work individually.
7. Increase the requirements for the numbers on the graphic organizer to include decimals or greater digits.

Resources:

Slideshow on Dewey Decimal System
http://www.breitlinks.com/dewey_for_kids.htm

Greater than, less than, and equal explanation
http://www.mathsisfun.com/equal-less-greater.html

Number sentences
http://www.icoachmath.com/math_dictionary/
  Number_Sentence.html

About number sentences
http://scimathmn.org/stemtc/frameworks/
  222-number-sentences

Review of math vocabulary with music and graphics
http://clubtnt.org/mathminutes/definitions_n_
  symbols.htm

Exemplar Texts:

On the Playground: How Do You Build Place Value?
By Donna Loughran. Norwood House, 2013. 24p.
  (9781599535494)
Grade Level: K–2
ATOS Reading Level: 3.1

previous understandings of operations on whole numbers.

Number and Operations in Base Ten

- Extend the counting sequence.
- Solve problems involving the four operations, and identify and explain patterns in arithmetic.
- Generalize place value understanding for multi-digit whole numbers.
- Use place value understanding and properties of operations to perform multi-digit arithmetic.
- Perform operations with multi-digit whole numbers and with decimals to hundredths.

Number and Operations—Fractions

- Develop understanding of fractions as numbers.
- Extend understanding of fraction equivalence and ordering.
- Understand decimal notation for fractions, and compare decimal fractions.

Measurement and Data

- Tell and write time.
- Work with time and money.
- Measure and estimate lengths in standard units.
- Describe and compare measurable attributes.

- Classify objects and count the number of objects in categories.
- Solve problems involving measurement and estimation of intervals of time, liquid volumes, and masses of objects.
- Represent and interpret data.

Lexile Level: AD 510L
Dewey: 519.5

One Is a Snail, Ten Is a Crab: A Counting by Feet Book.
By April Pulley Sayre and Jeff Sayre. Candlewick, 2006. 40p. (9780763626310)
Grade Level: PreK–2
Lexile Level: 1520L
Dewey: E

The Great Dewey Hunt.
By Toni Buzzeo. Upstart Books, 2009. 36p. (9781602130296)
Grade Level: K–3
ATOS Reading Level: 3.7
Dewey: E

The Shelf Elf Helps Out.
By Jackie Mims Hopkins. Upstart Books, 2006. 36p. (9781932146455)
Grade Level: K–3
ATOS Reading Level: 4.3
Dewey: E

Zero the Hero.
By Joan Holub. Henry Holt, 2012. 40p. (9780805093841)
Grade Level: 1–5
ATOS Reading Level: 2.7
Lexile Level: 450L
Dewey: E

PART VI

Appendix: Graphic Organizers

Name_____ Date _____

GO Chart
A VERY IMPROBABLE STORY

Spin Number	Predicted Color	Spin Color	Correct
1.			
2.			
3.			
4.			
5.			
6.			
7.			
8.			
9.			
10.			

Pattern of probability: _____

_____

_____

_____

_____

Number sentence: _____

_____

_____

_____

_____

From *Teaching STEM and Common Core with Mentor Texts: Collaborative Lesson Plans, K–5* by Anastasia Suen and Shirley Duke. Santa Barbara, CA: Libraries Unlimited. Copyright © 2014.

Name_____ Date _____

AMAZING AMUSEMENT PARK RIDES

Name That Coaster!

The Roller Coaster	Steel Dragon	Your Coaster _____
Length of track		
Highest track height		
Speed		
Car Train Length		
Car Train Width		
Passengers per Train		
Number of Passengers (total per ride)		

Your Coaster Plans

Number of trips per hour: _____

Number of riders per trip: _____

Number of riders per hour: _____

Collected money per one trip: _____

Collected money per hour: _____

Collected money for the day: _____

Name_____ Date_____

GO Chart
ANIMALS AND THE ENVIRONMENT
Text Features

Facts	Text Features	Adaptations
Animal #1		
Animal #2		
Animal #3		

From *Teaching STEM and Common Core with Mentor Texts: Collaborative Lesson Plans, K–5* by Anastasia Suen and Shirley Duke. Santa Barbara, CA: Libraries Unlimited. Copyright © 2014.

Name _____ Date _____

GO Chart
BUILD IT

Go BATS for Bridge Supports

1. **B**eams
2. **A**rches
3. **T**russes
4. **S**uspension

Name_____ Date _____

GO Chart
COOL ENGINEERING ACTIVITIES FOR GIRLS (AND BOYS)
Use with collaborative teacher activity.

Distances

Names	Standard	Metric
1.		
2.		
3.		
4.		
5.		
6.		
7.		
8.		
9.		
10.		
11.		
12.		
13.		
14.		
15.		
16.		
17.		
18.		
19.		
20.		
21.		

From *Teaching STEM and Common Core with Mentor Texts: Collaborative Lesson Plans, K–5* by Anastasia Suen and Shirley Duke. Santa Barbara, CA: Libraries Unlimited. Copyright © 2014.

Name_____ Date_____

GO Chart

CRANES

Simple Machines

Diagram	**Example**
Definition	**2 Vocabulary Words**

Name_____ Date_____

GO Chart
CRANES

Simple Machines Notes

inclined plan

wedge

screw

lever

pulley

wheel and axle

From *Teaching STEM and Common Core with Mentor Texts: Collaborative Lesson Plans, K–5* by Anastasia Suen and Shirley Duke. Santa Barbara, CA: Libraries Unlimited. Copyright © 2014.

Name_____ Date_____

GO Chart
ENTERPRISE STEM

Technology:_____

1. An early inventor who developed your technology

_____

_____

_____

2. Description of what the early product looked like

_____

_____

_____

3. A description of its size then

_____

_____

_____

4. Changes in your technology over the years

_____

_____

_____

5. An explanation about why you think the inventor first made it or why this person thought it was needed

_____

_____

_____

Name_____ Date _____

GO Chart
FOR GOOD MEASURE

Measuring in Feet

Student Name	Your Feet		Actual Feet	
	Width	Length	Width	Length
1.				
2.				
3.				
4.				
5.				
6.				
7.				
8.				
9.				
10.				

From *Teaching STEM and Common Core with Mentor Texts: Collaborative Lesson Plans, K–5* by Anastasia Suen and Shirley Duke. Santa Barbara, CA: Libraries Unlimited. Copyright © 2014.

Name_____ Date_____

GO Chart
FORCES AND MOTION AT WORK
Forces and Motion Vocabulary

accelerate _____

aerodynamics _____

centrifugal force _____

centripetal force _____

deform _____

drag _____

electromagnets _____

forces _____

friction _____

gravity _____

inertia _____

kinetic energy _____

magnets _____

mechanics _____

potential energy _____

recoil _____

resistance _____

Name_____ Date_____

GO Chart
HIGH-TECH OLYMPICS

Sports Data

2008 Sport	Men	Women
high jump		
pole vault		
long jump		
triple jump		
shot put		
javelin		

Name of Sport: _____

1st Place Winners	Year	Country	Time/Distance
1.			
2.			
3.			
4.			
5.			

From *Teaching STEM and Common Core with Mentor Texts: Collaborative Lesson Plans, K–5* by Anastasia Suen and Shirley Duke. Santa Barbara, CA: Libraries Unlimited. Copyright © 2014.

GO Chart

HOW MANY JELLY BEANS?

Jelly Beans

_____   _____

_____   _____

_____   _____

_____   _____

_____   _____

_____   _____

_____   _____

_____   _____

_____   _____

_____   _____

_____   _____

_____   _____

_____   _____

_____   _____

_____   _____

Name_____ Date _____

INFINITY AND ME

Cutting to Infinity Data Table

Cuts	Length Before Cutting	Cut Length
1.		
2.		
3.		
4.		
5.		
6.		
7.		
8.		
9.		
10.		
11.		
12.		
13.		
14.		
15.		
16.		
17.		
18.		
19.		
20.		

From *Teaching STEM and Common Core with Mentor Texts: Collaborative Lesson Plans, K–5* by Anastasia Suen and Shirley Duke. Santa Barbara, CA: Libraries Unlimited. Copyright © 2014.

Name_____ Date _____

GO Chart

MAN ON THE MOON

Changes in Space Travel

Then	Now

Name_____ Date _____

GO Chart

MISSING MATH

Detective Search List

From your section, find five different books that have the following:

1. one book that contains a three-digit number
2. one more book that has a three-digit number
3. one book that has a number with one digit
4. one book that has a number with two digits
5. one book with the largest number you can find

Book Title	Author	Number Location
1.		
2.		
3.		
4.		
5.		

Name_____ Date _____

GO Chart
MULTIMEDIA ARTIST AND ANIMATOR
Response Sheet

1. I, We chose the abstract image because _____
   or
   I, We chose the face and background image because

   _____

2. The characteristics I, we added included the following:

   _____

3. I, We used these characteristics because

   _____

4. The final image looked like

   _____

5. The final animated picture did these things:

   _____

6. The final image made me, us feel

   _____

7. My, our art might possibly be used in

   _____

8. Think of a way that could use the kind of art you created and explain how it would work.

   _____

9. What might you change if you did this activity again?

   _____

10. What were the best and hardest parts of making art using technology?

   _____

Name_____ Date_____

GO Chart
OCEANS AND SEAS

Ecosystem: _____

Facts:

1. _____
_____

2. _____
_____

3. _____
_____

4. _____
_____

5. _____
_____

6. _____
_____

7. _____
_____

8. _____
_____

9. _____
_____

10. _____
_____

Sources:

_____
_____
_____

From *Teaching STEM and Common Core with Mentor Texts: Collaborative Lesson Plans, K–5* by Anastasia Suen and Shirley Duke. Santa Barbara, CA: Libraries Unlimited. Copyright © 2014.

Name_____ Date _____

GO Chart
PLANTING THE WILD GARDEN

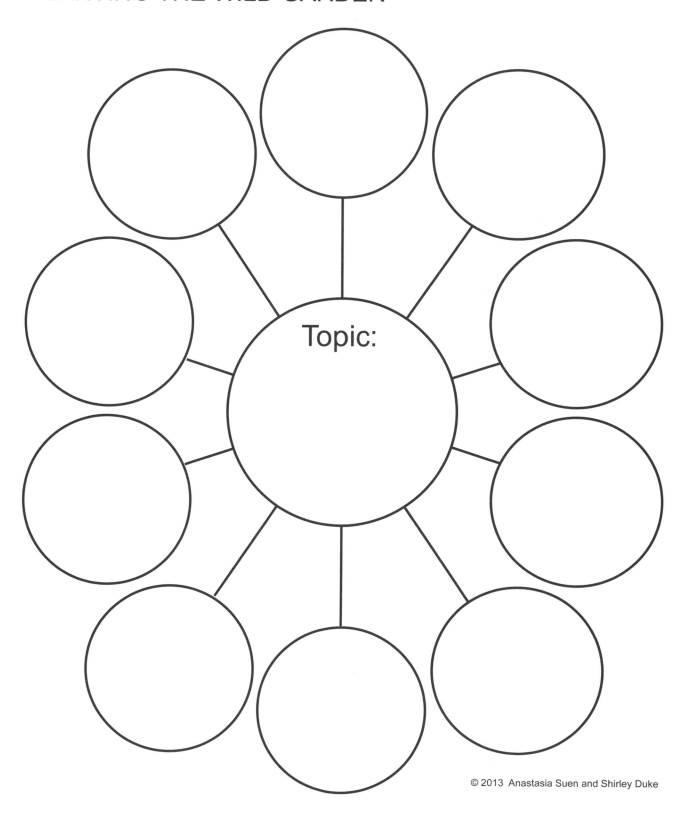

Topic:

Name_____ Date _____

GO Chart
POP! THE INVENTION OF BUBBLE GUM
Pop!

Step 1: What was Walter's problem?

Step 2: What did people know about gum and who needs bubble gum?

Step 3: What must bubble gum be like to be successful?

Step 4: How can we solve the problem of making bubble gum? Try these: (write as many ways as you can that Walter tried).

Step 5: What changes did Walter make to his bubble gum?

Step 6: What did he do to make the gum and how did he test it?

Step 7: What changes did he make in his gum after the test?

Step 8: How did Walter let people know about his bubble gum?

Name_____ Date_____

ROCKS AND MINERALS

Kinds of Rocks

Sedimentary	Igneous	Metamorphic
1.		
2.		
3.		

Name_____ Date _____

GO Chart

THE SHOCKING TRUTH ABOUT ENERGY

Energy

Energy Source	How it's Helpful	How it's Harmful
petroleum (oil)		
natural gas		
nuclear power		
solar power		
wind		
water (hydroelectric)		
geothermal		
plant power (biofuels)		

From *Teaching STEM and Common Core with Mentor Texts: Collaborative Lesson Plans, K–5* by Anastasia Suen and Shirley Duke. Santa Barbara, CA: Libraries Unlimited. Copyright © 2014.

Name_____ Date _____

GO Chart
WIRED

Wired Main Ideas

Pages 2-3	_____
Pages 4-5	_____
Pages 6-7	_____
Pages 8-9	_____
Pages 10-11	_____
Pages 12-13	_____
Pages 14-15	_____
Pages 16-17	_____
Pages 18-19	_____
Pages 20-21	_____
Pages 22-23	_____
Pages 24-25	_____
Pages 26-27	_____
Pages 28-29	_____
Pages 30-31	_____
Page 32	_____

Flow Chart Notes

_____
_____
_____
_____
_____
_____
_____

Bibliography

"All Aboard!: Implementing Common Core Offers School Librarians an Opportunity to Take the Lead: School Library Journal." *School Library Journal: The World's Largest Reviewer of Books, Multimedia, and Technology for Children and Teens.* http://www.schoollibraryjournal.com/slj/printissue/currentissue/893928-427/all_aboard_implementing_common_core.html.csp (accessed August 9, 2013).

Duff, Marina. "Supporting STEM Studies in Secondary Public School Libraries." *STEM Libraries.* www.lausd.net/Young_Oak_Kim_Academy/YOKA/Resources_files/STEM%20Libraries.pdf (accessed August 9, 2013).

"English Language Arts: American Association of School Librarians (AASL)." *American Library Association.* http://www.ala.org/aasl/guidelinesandstandards/commoncorecrosswalk/english (accessed August 9, 2013).

"Find a Book—The Lexile Framework for Reading." The Lexile Framework for Reading. http://www.lexile.com/fab/ (accessed August 9, 2013).

Garrett, Ron V., CEO, and Parent-Teacher Association. "The National Governors Association Center for Best Practices (NGA Center) and the Council of Chief State School Officers (CCSSO)." The Council of Chief State School Officers. http://www.ccsso.org/News_and_Events/Press_Releases/NATIONAL_GOVERNORS_ASSOCIATION_AND_STATE_EDUCATION_CHIEFS_LAUNCH_COMMON_STATE_ACADEMIC_STANDARDS_.html (accessed August 9, 2013).

Gerlach, Jonathan. "NSTA Reports." *STEM: Defying a Simple Definition.* 2012. http://www.nsta.org/publications/news/story.aspx?id=59305 (accessed August 9, 2013).

Hallinen, Judith, Ross MacConnell, and Richard Wang. "Report of a Project to Identify STEM Education in Southwestern Pennsylvania." www.cmu.edu/gelfand/documents/stem-survey-report-cmu-iu1.pdf (accessed August 9, 2013).

Lantz, Hayes. "Science, Technology, Engineering, and Mathematics (STEM) Education: What Form? What Function?: What is STEM Education." www.currtechintegrations.com/pdf/STEMEducationArticle.pdf (accessed August 9, 2013).

"Nature of Science." Home: UB Graduate School of Education. http://gse.buffalo.edu/fas/shuell/cep564/Science.htm (accessed August 9, 2013).

Renaissance Learning. "AR Book Finder." *AR Book Finder.* http://www.arbookfind.com/ (accessed August 9, 2013).

Rutherford, James, and Andrew Ahlgren. "Chapter 3: The Nature of Technology." AAAS—Project 2061. http://www.project2061.org/publications/sfaa/online/chap3.htm (accessed August 9, 2013).

Science Buddies. "The Engineering Design Process." The Engineering Design Process. www.sciencebuddies.org/engineering-design-process/engineering-design-process-steps.shtml (accessed August 9, 2013).

Silvaroli, Nicholas Joseph. *Classroom Reading Inventory*. 2d ed. Dubuque, Iowa: W.C. Brown Co., 1973.

"What Is Mathematics?" U.S. Department of Education. http://www2.ed.gov/pubs/EarlyMath/whatis.html (accessed August 9, 2013).

Title Index

Subject Index

About the Authors

ANASTASIA SUEN has taught kindergarten to college. The prolific author of over one hundred and sixty books and the founder of STEM Friday, she writes about science, technology, engineering, and mathematics for children, teens, and adults. Her recent books include *Online Privacy and the Law, Internships and Volunteer Opportunities for People Who Love All Things Digital,* and *The Fossil Hunt.*

SHIRLEY DUKE has taught science for twenty-five years at the elementary and secondary levels. She's written over thirty science books for children. Her most recent books include the Seasons of the Biomes series for Rourke Educational Media, 2013. She holds a bachelor's degree in biology and a master's degree in education from Austin College in Sherman, Texas.